OECD Green Growth Studies

Green Growth Indicators for Agriculture

A PRELIMINARY ASSESSMENT

This work is published under the responsibility of the Secretary-General of the OECD. The opinions expressed and arguments employed herein do not necessarily reflect the official views of OECD member countries.

This document and any map included herein are without prejudice to the status of or sovereignty over any territory, to the delimitation of international frontiers and boundaries and to the name of any territory, city or area.

Please cite this publication as:
OECD (2014), *Green Growth Indicators for Agriculture: A Preliminary Assessment*, OECD Green Growth Studies, OECD Publishing.
http://dx.doi.org/10.1787/9789264223202-en

ISBN 978-92-64-22317-2 (print)
ISBN 978-92-64-22320-2 (PDF)

Series: OECD Green Growth Studies
ISSN 2222-9515 (print)
ISSN 2222-9523 (online)

The statistical data for Israel are supplied by and under the responsibility of the relevant Israeli authorities. The use of such data by the OECD is without prejudice to the status of the Golan Heights, East Jerusalem and Israeli settlements in the West Bank under the terms of international law.

Foreword

As part of its *Green Growth Strategy*, the OECD has developed a conceptual framework to monitor economic growth and development, while combating climate change and preventing the inefficient use of natural resources and environmental degradation.

This report presents the work undertaken to identify the relevant and measurable indicators for the agricultural sector in alignment with the OECD's *Green Growth Measurement Framework*. These indicators have been then calculated and applied to a selected number of OECD countries in three specific policy areas: the transition to a low-carbon, resource-efficient agricultural sector; the maintenance of a natural asset base; and the implementation of policies aimed at realising the economic opportunities associated with green growth in the agricultural sector.

While most green growth indicators overlap with existing indicators of agricultural policy support, agri-environmental and agricultural commodity indicators, or can be derived from OECD and other economic and environmental statistics, they do not necessarily capture the dynamics of green growth in agriculture and present these in terms of quantifiable indicators that can be unambiguously interpreted and easily communicated to policy makers.

Establishing quantitative assessments of the cause and effect linkages between a country's policies and its green growth performance is a difficult task given the context-specific nature of many environmental issues, the varying preferences constituting green growth across countries, the multiple factors determining environmental outcomes in agriculture, and the lack of objective valuations of environmental externalities and public goods. Any comparisons across countries would need to be undertaken with great caution, but comparison of trends over time could provide useful insights and provide an important focus to monitor progress towards green growth.

This work represents a first step in the further development and refinement of green growth indicators in agriculture. New indicators continue to be developed by the OECD to provide governments with a full range of green growth indicators in agriculture. Gaps in methodology, concepts and data also continue to be addressed.

This report was prepared by the OECD's Trade and Agriculture Directorate (TAD) and has benefited from the expert advice of other Directorates, in particular the Environment Directorate, the Statistics Directorate, the Economics Department, and the Centre on Tax Policy and Administration. It was declassified by the OECD Joint Working Party on Agriculture and the Environment in April 2014.

Dimitris Diakosavvas is the author of this report, which was declassified by the Joint Working Party on Agriculture and the Environment under the title *Monitoring Progress Towards Green Growth in Agriculture: Preliminary Results*. It was prepared for publication by Françoise Bénicourt and Michèle Patterson. Valuable assistance was also provided by Theresa Poincet, Noura Takrouri-Jolly and Véronique de Saint-Martin.

Table of contents

Abbreviations 9

Main online data sources 11

Executive summary 13

Chapter 1 Conceptual considerations to greening agricultural growth 15

    The OECD green growth measurement framework 17
    Selecting policy-relevant indicators for agriculture 19
    Proposed indicators and caveats 21
    Note 23
    Bibliography 24

Chapter 2 Contextual indicators for agricultural growth 25

    Measurability 26
    Main trends 27
    Bibliography 36

Chapter 3 Monitoring the environmental efficiency and natural resource productivity
of agriculture 37

    Carbon productivity 41
    Energy productivity 45
    Water use intensity 48
    Nutrient flows and balances 50
    Material productivity (biomass) 54
    Environmentally adjusted total factor productivity 55
    Notes 56
    Bibliography 58

Chapter 4 Monitoring the impact of agriculture on the natural asset base and environmental
quality of life 59

    Renewable stocks: Freshwater 61
    Biodiversity and ecosystems 63
    Note 66
    Bibliography 67

Chapter 5 Monitoring policy responses and economic opportunities in agriculture 69

    Monitoring policy responses 72
    Monitoring economic opportunities 82
    Notes 93
    Bibliography 95

Tables

Table 1.1. Agricultural-related indicators used by the Czech Republic, Korea and the Netherlands...17

Table 1.2. Synopsis of the proposed list of indicators...22

Table 2.1. Measuring the economic performance of agriculture...26

Table 3.1. Environmental efficiency and natural resource productivity/intensity indicators......40

Table 4.1. Indicators for monitoring the natural asset base...60

Table 5.1. Green growth toolkit for food and agriculture 71

Table 5.2. Indicators for monitoring green growth policies and opportunities 73

Table 5.3. Full supply cost recovery for surface water delivered on-farm in OECD countries, 2008..81

Table 5.4. Training and education in agriculture in selected OECD countries, 2005 and 2010 (%)..85

Table 5.5. Share of young and elderly farmers in some EU member states, 1990, 2007 and 2010...87

Figures

Figure 1.1. OECD green growth measurement framework 18

Figure 1.2. Green growth indicator groups and themes..18

Figure 2.1. Agriculture's contribution to the economy, 2010 or latest.....................................27

Figure 2.2. Importance of agricultural trade in OECD countries, 2010....................................28

Figure 2.3. Participation and position in GVCs for agriculture and food products, 2009 29

Figure 2.4. Average annual growth in agricultural production volume, 1990-2011 (%)............30

Figure 2.5. Total factor productivity (TFP) of agriculture, annual growth rates (%) 32

Figure 2.6. Cereal yield growth rates, 1990-2011 (%) 32

Figure 2.7. Agricultural labour productivity growth rates, 1990-2010 (%)..............................33

Figure 2.8. Agricultural investment productivity growth, 1990-2007 (1990=100)....................33

Figure 2.9. Evolution of primary commodity prices 34

Figure 3.1. Stylised representation of resource and impact decoupling 39

Figure 3.2. Share of agriculture in total GHG emissions, 2008-10 (%) 42

Figure 3.3. GHG emissions from agriculture in the OECD area, by source, 2008-10 (%).............43

Figure 3.4. Growth rate of total economy and agricultural net GHG emissions 43

Figure 3.5. GHG emissions, GDP and productivity for agriculture in the OECD area...................44

Figure 3.6. Agricultural economic growth and GHG emissions and relation with decoupling, 1990-2010 44

Figure 3.7. Agricultural GHG emissions productivity, 2008-10 45

Figure 3.8. Agricultural GHG emissions productivity by source in the OECD area.....................45

Figure 3.9. Direct on-farm energy productivity, OECD area 47

Figure 3.10. Direct on-farm energy productivity, 2009-10 47

Figure 3.11. Agricultural water use intensity versus irrigated area 49

Figure 3.12. Share of irrigated area 49

Figure 3.13. Nutrient balances intensity and agricultural production, OECD area (1990=100) 51

Figure 3.14. Nutrient decoupling trends..52

Figure 3.15. Apparent consumption and intensity of inorganic fertilisers, and crop production, OECD area 52

Figure 3.16. Decoupling trends of inorganic fertilisers 53

Figure 3.17. Nutrient intensities per area of agricultural land, 2008-09 (kg/ha) 54

Figure 4.1. Agricultural water withdrawals in selected OECD countries 62
Figure 4.2. Trends in agricultural land cover, change over the period 1990-2010
or most recent year 65
Figure 4.3. Farmland bird index in selected countries 66
Figure 5.1. Evolution of producer support by potential environmental impact in the OECD area .. 76
Figure 5.2. Producer support by potential environmental impact in OECD countries 77
Figure 5.3. Environmental taxes in agriculture 78
Figure 5.4. Environmental taxes in agriculture by type: Share in total (%), 2010
or most recent year 79
Figure 5.5. Tax rates on energy and CO_2 from energy 80
Figure 5.6. Evolution of payments on agricultural schools and total support to agriculture,
OECD area 86
Figure 5.7. Government budget appropriations or outlays for R&D (GBAORD): Share of
agriculture, 2010-12, (%) 88
Figure 5.8. Business enterprises R&D expenditure: Share of agriculture in total,
2010 or more recent year 88
Figure 5.9. Share of agricultural R&D payments in total support to agriculture, 2010-12 89
Figure 5.10. Evolution of agricultural R&D payments and total support to agriculture,
OECD area 89
Figure 5.11. Main scientific fields cited in green patents, by inventor country, 2000-07 90
Figure 5.12. Patents in environment-related technologies in agriculture, OECD area (1999=100) .. 91
Figure 5.13. Patents in environmentally-related technologies in agriculture, 2008-10 92
Figure 5.14. Trends of water-related innovations in agriculture 93

Boxes

Box 2.1. Measuring trade in value added 28
Box 3.1. The resource productivity concept 38
Box 3.2. Decoupling concepts 39
Box 3.3. OECD's on-going work on adjusting total factor productivity estimates
to account for environmental services 56

Abbreviations

CBD	Convention on Biological Diversity
CH_4	Methane
CO_2	Carbon dioxide
CSE	Consumer support estimate
DMC	Domestic material consumption
DMI	Domestic material input
EEA	European Environment Agency
EUR	Euro
FAO	Food and Agriculture Organization of the United Nations
GBAORD	Government budget appropriations on R&D
GDP	Gross domestic product
GHG	Greenhouse gas
GJ	Gigajoules
GVC	Global value chain
ha	hectare
IEA	International Energy Agency
IMF	International Monetary Fund
IPCC	Intergovernmental Panel on Climate Change
ISIC	International Standard Industrial Classification
IUCN	International Union for Conservation of Nature
LULUCF	Land use, land use-change and forestry
MFA	Material flow analysis
N	Nitrogen
N_2O	Nitrogen oxide
NPL	Non-patent literature
P	Phosphorus
PCT	Patent Cooperation Treaty
PSE	Producer support estimate
TFP	Total factor productivity
SEEA	System of Environmental-Economic Accounting
UNEP	UN Environment Programme
UNFCCC	United Nations Framework Convention on Climate Change
USD	US dollar
WAVES	Wealth accounting and valuation of ecosystem services

Main online data sources

EUROSTAT

Farm structures, http://epp.eurostat.ec.europa.eu/portal/page/portal/statistics/search_database

FAO

FAOSTAT, http://faostat3.fao.org/faostat-gateway/go/to/home/E

OECD

Producer and consumer support estimates, *OECD Agriculture Statistics,* www.oecd.org/agriculture/agricultural-policies/producerandconsumersupportestimatesdatabase.htm.

Agri-environmental indicators, *OECD Agriculture Statistics*, http://dx.doi.org/10.1787/agr-aei-data-en.

Research and Development Statistics, *OECD Science, Technology and R&D Statistics*, http://dx.doi.org/10.1787/1996305x.

Patent Statistics, http://dx.doi.org/10.1787/patent-data-en.

Productivity Statistics, http://dx.doi.org/10.1787/pdtvy-data-en.

Global Value Chain Indicators, http://stats.oecd.org/Index.aspx?DataSetCode=GVC_INDICATORS

Selected green growth indicators, http://stats.oecd.org/Index.aspx?DataSetCode=GREEN_GROWTH.

OECD/EEA

http://www2.oecd.org/ecoinst/queries/

International Energy Agency (IEA)

Energy Statistics *of OECD Countries 2012*, OECD Publishing, Paris, http://dx.doi.org/10.1787/energy_stats_oecd-2012-en

International Fertilizer Industry Association (IFA)

Fertiliser Statistics, http://www.fertilizer.org/Statistics

International Monetary Fund (IMF)

Primary Commodity Prices, http://www.imf.org/external/np/res/commod/index.aspx

UN Framework Convention on Climate Change (UNFCCC)

GHG inventory data, http://unfccc.int/ghg_data/items/3800.php

World Bank

World Development Indicators, http://data.worldbank.org/data-catalog/world-development-indicators

Executive summary

An integral component of any green growth strategy is a reliable set of measurement tools and indicators to evaluate the effectiveness of policies and to gauge the progress achieved in shifting economic activity towards a greener path. These tools and indicators must be based on internationally comparable data and integrated within a conceptual framework. It is necessary also to select indicators according to a specific set of criteria.

This report is a first step in developing the *OECD Green Growth Strategy Measurement Framework* that will monitor progress on green growth in the agricultural sector of OECD countries. The goal is to identify the relevant, succinct and measurable statistics that will provide the basis to further develop green growth indicators in this sector. It analyses what is needed and how to build on the available data in terms of economic performance indicators, policy indicators and agri-environmental indicators.

A preliminary selection of indicators has been made on the basis of existing work undertaken by the OECD and other international organisations, and they have been structured in line with the *OECD Green Growth Strategy Measurement Framework*. The choice of specific indicators was governed by the idea of capturing key aspects of a low-carbon, resource-efficient agricultural sector. More specifically, it was based on the following guiding principles:

- Provide a balanced coverage of the two dimensions of green growth – "green" and "growth" – and of their main elements, with particular attention given to indicators capturing the interface between the two.

- Measurable and comparable across countries.

- Reflect key issues of common relevance to green growth in OECD countries.

- Easy to communicate.

- Aligned with the OECD measurement framework for green growth.

These criteria are not new, but rather variations of more specific aspects of OECD basic guiding principles for indicators concerning policy relevance, analytical soundness and measurability.

In addition to the aforementioned key guiding principles, two other criteria have been used in this study:

- Adjustment of indicators to relate them to national green growth approaches and strategies used by OECD countries.

- Indicators were constructed based on existing data sources.

A preliminary selection of approximately 25 indicators was made to assess green growth progress in the agricultural sector. They were derived from existing databases of the OECD (i.e. the Producer and Consumer Support, agri-environmental indicators, productivity statistics and patent statistical databases), the FAO, the World Bank (World Development Indicators database) and EUROSTAT.

A far greater range of indicators can be constructed from these databases, but the focus here is on the key aspects of green growth in agriculture for which it is feasible to consistently develop suitable indicators over time. This list is sufficiently flexible to enable countries to adapt it to its national context.

Priority areas for progress

The list of the proposed indicators will be further developed as new data become available and existing concepts evolve. In particular, progress in this area will benefit greatly from work currently being undertaken by OECD on advancing the green growth measurement agenda, on the completion and implementation of the United Nations' Integrated *System of Environmental-Economic Accounting* (SEEA), and by the World Bank-led *Wealth Accounting and Valuation of Ecosystem Services* (WAVES) partnership.

Specific priority areas for follow-up work to address important methodological and data gaps include the following areas:

- Including natural assets in growth accounting, and thereby derive new measures of total-factor productivity growth.

- Development of indicators for regulatory instruments, which are more complicated than those on economic instruments (e.g. government transfers and taxes). Careful consideration should be given to how indicators on policy responses can be complemented by indicators on environmental regulations, which are very important for the agricultural sector in most OECD countries.

- Improving the data on water pricing and cost recovery.

- Further improving green-related R&D and innovation data in agriculture.

Chapter 1

Conceptual considerations to greening agricultural growth

The OECD conceptual framework for monitoring progress towards green growth focuses on the environmental performance of production and consumption, and on the key drivers of green growth, such as policy instruments and innovation. This chapter briefly describes the OECD conceptual framework and the general principles used to select relevant indicators to monitor progress towards green growth in agriculture. It also provides a synopsis of the proposed indicators.

Green growth is defined as fostering economic growth and development, while sustaining the natural assets base that provides the resources and environmental services on which we rely for our well-being (OECD, 2011a). In response to the global economic downturn as well as recognising that there are biophysical limits to growth, the green growth agenda places renewed focus on the fundamental drivers of growth, including the use of factors of production, environmental innovation and the removal of policy distortions. A green growth strategy can generate a "double dividend" effect – higher growth with lower adverse environmental impact – by improving the efficiency of resource use and increasing investments in natural capital to drive economic growth (OECD, 2011a).

Policies that promote green growth need to be supported with appropriate measurement tools to monitor progress and gauge how well policies are performing in shifting economic activity to a greener path. Green growth indicators can help identify policy opportunities that can improve growth and environmental outcomes, or to identify policies that can address possible trade-offs between green and growth objectives.

Reporting and measuring the progress of green growth is important for the work on policy undertaken by the OECD, other international organisations. The OECD has developed, *inter alia*, a conceptual measurement framework and set of indicators to help governments monitor progress towards green growth (OECD, 2011b*); UNEP has developed indicators for green economy policy making (UNEP 2012a, 2012b and 2012c); the World Bank has developed a framework to measure the potential benefits from green growth policies (World Bank, 2012); and the European Commission has developed a *Roadmap to a Resource Efficient Europe* (EC, 2011).

Green growth indicators are used in the OECD to incorporate green growth into its core policy advice. Two areas where green growth indicators figure prominently are the OECD's *Environmental Performance Reviews* and the *Economic Country Surveys*. Member countries, such as the Czech Republic, Germany, Korea, Mexico, the Slovak Republic and the Netherlands, have already applied the OECD green growth measurement framework to their national economy and produced their own indicator reports using national data. Some of these country reports also include agriculture-related indicators (**Table 1.1**). Similar work is underway in non-member countries, such as Colombia, Costa Rica, Ecuador, Guatemala, Paraguay, Peru and Kyrgyzstan.

The OECD green growth indicator report, *Towards Green Growth: Monitoring Progress – OECD Indicators*, is regularly updated as new data become available (OECD, 2011b; 2014). A green growth indicators database has been created; it contains selected indicators to monitor green growth progress to support policy making and inform the public at large. The dataset covers OECD countries, as well as BRIICS economies (Brazil, Russian Federation, India, Indonesia, China and South Africa), Argentina and Saudi Arabia from 1990 to the most recent years available.

The main objective of this report, therefore, is to develop this framework for the agricultural sector and apply it to selected OECD countries.[1] In particular, it analyses what is needed and then how to build on what we have in terms of economic performance, policy and agri-environmental indicators in order to develop a set of green growth indicators for agriculture.

Table 1.1. Agriculture-related indicators used in the Czech Republic, Korea, the Netherlands and the Slovak Republic

	Environmental and resource productivity	Natural resource base
Czech Republic	Nutrient balances: • nitrogen • phosphorus	Land cover change: • agricultural land, pastures and meadows • urban areas and infrastructure • semi-natural habitats Farmland birds
Korea	Consumption of chemical fertilisers	Annual rainfall per capita
Netherlands	Energy efficiency: • agriculture • manufacturing • transport • other services Share of renewable energy in total: • biomass • wind • other Nutrient balances: • nitrogen • phosphorus	Land conversion into built-up land: • agriculture • nature • forest • built-up
Slovak Republic	Nutrient balances	Land use Agricultural land area affected by water and wind erosion, by class of erosion

Source: OECD (2013), *Policy Instruments to Support Green Growth in Agriculture*, OECD Green Growth Studies, OECD Publishing.
doi: 10.1787/9789264203525-en.

The OECD green growth measurement framework

The cornerstone of the OECD approach to monitor progress towards green growth is a conceptual framework that reflects the integrated nature of green growth and describes the main aspects that need to be monitored. This approach reflects a production framework of the economic growth theory model, whereby inputs are transformed into outputs. It draws on groups of indicators which capture major aspects of green growth. Particular attention is given to efficiency and productivity issues. The focus is on the environmental performance of production and consumption, and on the drivers of green growth, such as policy instruments and innovation activity (**Figure 1.1** and **Figure 1.2**).

Figure 1.1. OECD green growth measurement framework

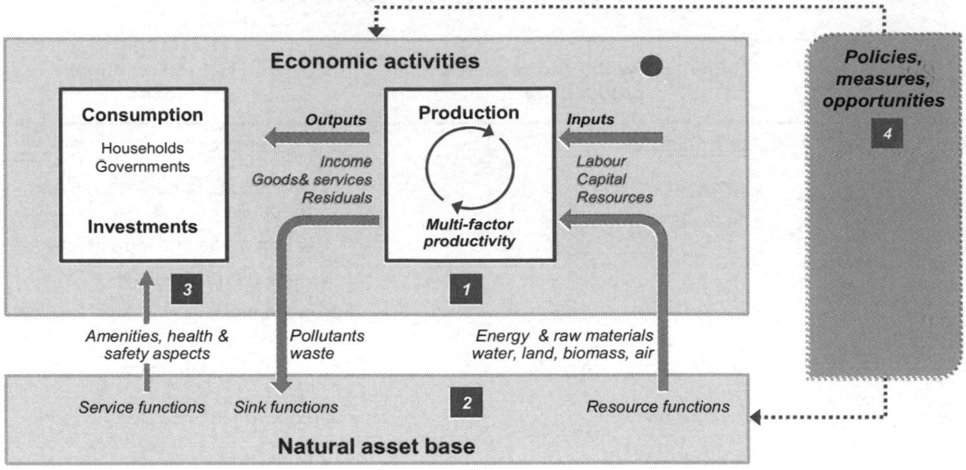

Source: OECD (2011), *Towards Green Growth*, OECD Green Growth Studies, OECD Publishing. doi: http://dx.doi.org/10.1787/9789264111318-en.

Figure 1.2. Green growth indicator groups and themes

1. The environmental and resource productivity of the economy	- Carbon and energy productivity - Resource productivity: materials, nutrients, water - Multi-factor productivity
2. The natural asset base	- Renewable stocks: water, forest, fish resources - Non-renewable stocks: mineral resources - Biodiversity and ecosystems
3. The environmental dimension of quality of life	- Environmental health and risks - Environmental services and amenities
4. Economic opportunities and policy responses	- Technology and innovation - Environmental goods and services - International financial flows - Prices and transfers - Skills and training - Regulations and management approaches
Socio-economic context and characteristics of growth	- Economic growth and structure - Productivity and trade - Labour markets, education and income - Socio-demographic patterns

Source: OECD (2011), *Towards Green Growth*, OECD Green Growth Studies, OECD Publishing. doi: 10.1787/9789264111318-en.

For each group, a list of indicators was proposed on the basis of existing OECD work and experience (OECD, 2011b; 2014). These four groups of indicators are complemented with generic indicators describing the socio-economic context and characteristics of growth.

This measurement framework was used to develop a proposed list of 25 green growth indicators for OECD countries (OECD, 2011b), originally presented in a 2011 report to ministers along with data for OECD and emerging economies. It was updated in 2014 (*Green Growth Indicators 2014*, OECD, 2014).

Selecting policy-relevant indicators for agriculture

Although the concept of "green growth" is relatively new, "green growth" indicators are not. Most overlap with existing sustainable development and environmental indicators or can be derived from economic, environmental and social statistics that have been collected and compiled by national statistical offices and other national and international bodies. Statistical activities to monitor a country's progress on green growth can thus be streamlined with existing activities related to social, environmental and economic policy priorities (e.g. national sustainable development strategies, economic-environmental accounting and environmental monitoring).

The OECD has considerable experience in monitoring and evaluating agricultural and agri-environmental policies and approaches. Various databases and indicators have been developed which are relevant to monitoring green growth in agriculture. Moreover, several initiatives have been carried out to foster the adoption of sustainability indicators – which can overlap with green growth indicators – into national and international policies, and data have been collected and organised into so-called "environmental accounts" to help track the potential impact of economic and human activity on the environment (e.g. SEEA).

Moreover, governments in several OECD countries are increasingly aware of the importance to monitor and evaluate their agricultural policies and are devoting considerable efforts to strengthening these. For example, evaluation of the EU's rural development programmes, which include agro-environmental programmes, is required by legislation within an established framework that comprises quantitative indicators. Less formal approaches are used by other member countries which also use quantitative indicators (OECD, 2009). In addition, several OECD countries have already implemented the OECD Green Growth measurement framework, and some include agriculture-related indicators (e.g. the Czech Republic, Korea, the Netherlands, the Slovak Republic) (OECD, 2013b).

Notwithstanding the experience gained and amount of data collected, there are no existing indicators for the agricultural sector that can track progress towards green growth. Creating a set of indicators to monitor and evaluate progress towards green growth in the agricultural sector is challenging because: 1) approaches that countries are taking towards green growth vary considerably; 2) environmental outcomes in agriculture are determined by multiple factors and there are methodological, measurement and data availability problems in evaluating the environmental impacts of polices; 3) many environmental issues are context-specific and there is no single overarching indicator of environmental performance; 4) not only are the links between the biophysical, economic and policy processes complex, but information on the state of the environment is difficult to collect and interpret; and 5) there is a lack of objective valuations of environmental externalities and public goods. It is therefore difficult to establish quantitative assessments of the cause and effect linkages between policies and green growth performance in a country, and any cross-country comparison would need to be undertaken with great caution (OECD, 2012).

With this in mind, an important consideration in drawing up a set of green growth indicators for agriculture is to identify guiding principles. Ideally, indicators would fulfil the following criteria.

Criterion 1: Capture the nexus between the environment and the economy

As green growth concerns the interaction between environment and the economy, a key element in the choice of a green growth indicator is that it should contain information about the economic growth of the sector and its sources. A key principle is to achieve a balanced coverage of the two dimensions of green growth – "green" and "growth" – and of their main determinants, with particular attention given to indicators capturing the interface between the two. Capturing this nexus is an important – if not the most important – criterion for the selection of a green growth indicator.

Tracking trends in decoupling economic growth from environmental pressures is an important focus and indicators measuring the relationship between growth and environmental impacts are crucial for monitoring green growth. However, while decoupling indicators show whether production has become greener in relative terms, they do not indicate whether pressure on environmental services is decreasing in absolute terms. Absolute decoupling indicators (i.e. the economic indicator is growing, while the environmental indicator is unchanged or decreasing) help to fill this gap, but need to be complemented with information on *absolute levels* of environmental services because of potential thresholds and non-linear changes in the environment. In the absence of such information, little can be said about what the "optimal" rate of decoupling for a given country is or whether the rate needs to be increased or decreased (OECD, 2014).

Criterion 2: Be measurable and comparable across countries

A valid indicator for the OECD must be measurable and applicable to a reasonable number of countries and at different time periods. Definitions and data need to allow for meaningful comparison both across time and countries or regions. Indicators should be based on available data, or that can be made available at a reasonable cost, and that are adequately documented and of known quality.

A related issue is the timeliness of data. One of the biggest challenges is that agri-environmental data and indicators are often not collected and disseminated with the same frequency and speed as the data and indicators on economic performance and on government transfers. An important consideration for an indicator is that it is (or can be) updated regularly.

Immediate measurability, however, is not a necessary condition for inclusion or exclusion of an indicator and some flexibility is required. If, for example, an indicator is considered analytically sound, policy-relevant and can be made available at a reasonable cost it should be included.

Criterion 3: Reflect key global environmental issues

The need to capture the intersection between the environmental and economic dimensions of agricultural production is balanced against the need for indicators to address those areas where environmental concern is greatest. Climate change, biodiversity loss and sustainable management of water resources are generally regarded to be major policy challenges facing both OECD and non-OECD countries. For climate change and energy use, several countries have set quantifiable targets (e.g. reduced greenhouse gases, increased energy efficiency and share of renewable energy) (OECD, 2013a). However, coverage of key global environmental issues should not be the sole selection criterion, especially if the indicator does not capture the link with economic growth.

Criterion 4: Ease of communication for different users and audiences

The definition and interpretation of an indicator must not be ambiguous. Indicators must be transparent and easy to interpret, and any change must be easily understood as being either good or bad for green growth. Ensuring that it is based on the best available science and is analytically sound are key features to ensure the indicator is valid.

Criterion 5: Alignment with the OECD Green Growth measurement framework

The point of departure for designing a sector-specific framework to monitor progress towards green growth in agriculture is the economy-wide framework and the list of green growth indicators developed by the OECD. As noted earlier, the measurement framework proposed by the OECD effectively captures the main dimensions of green growth. Thus, the indicators chosen should be consistent with the OECD framework and should be able to track the economic and environmental performance of the agricultural sector.

In addition to the aforementioned guiding principles, two other criteria have been used in the current exercise:

- Adjustment of indicators to relate them to the national green growth approaches and strategies discussed in the *Policy Instruments to Support Green Growth in Agriculture; A Synthesis of Country Experiences* (OECD, 2013a).

- Indicators should, to the extent possible, be developed based on existing OECD work as well as data from other international organisations.

Proposed indicators and caveats

Given its multidimensional nature, green growth is not adequately captured by a single indicator. For OECD countries, a wide range of indicators related to economic and environmental performance of the agricultural sector as well as indicators describing the policy environment governing the sector should be developed. However, capturing the dynamics of green growth in agriculture and presenting them in terms of quantifiable indicators that could be interpreted unambiguously and easily communicated to policy makers remains a challenging task.

To monitor progress, a small set of indicators able to track the central elements of green growth issues associated with the agricultural sector across OECD member countries is proposed and applied to selected OECD countries. The proposed indicators constitute work in progress and will be further elaborated by OECD over time as data become available and as concepts evolve.

Table 1.2 provides a synopsis of the proposed indicators; the full list is provided by group in each relevant chapter. The proposed set of indicators is comprised of approximately 25 indicators, not all of which are yet measurable. At this stage, only three indicators fulfil all criteria: the indicators related to carbon and energy productivity, and the one related to the potentially most environmentally harmful producer support.

There are important caveats concerning this list. First, the set of indicators is limited in number. It represents a first selection made on the basis of existing work by OECD and member countries' experiences with green growth in agriculture. Gaps exist, both in terms of data availability and quality, as well at the conceptual level.

Table 1.2. Synopsis of the proposed list of indicators

Topic or issue	Criteria			
	Capturing the nexus between the environment and the economy	Ease of communication to different users and audiences	Reflecting key global environmental issues	Measurable and comparable across countries
Environmental efficiency				
Carbon productivity	***	***	***	***
Nutrient balance intensities	***	***	***	*
Resource efficiency				
Energy productivity	***	***	***	***
Renewable energy	***	***	***	*
Water productivity	***	***	***	*
Material (biomass) productivity	Indicators to be developed			
Environmentally-adjusted multi-factor productivity	***	**	***	*
Natural asset base				
Changes in agricultural land use and cover	***	***	***	**
Environmental quality of life	No indicator is proposed			
Economic opportunities and policy responses				
Potentially most environmentally harmful producer support	***	***	***	***
Environment-related taxes	***	***	***	**
Water pricing	***	***	**	*
Empowering people to innovate in agriculture	***	***		**
Environment-related innovation in agriculture	***	**	***	*
Regulatory instruments	Indicators to be developed			

Secondly, not all of the proposed indicators are relevant across all countries. The emphasis will vary, depending on the overall development status and priorities/particularities of a given country. National circumstances such as socio-economic structure, geography and climate will also influence the relevance, selection and interpretation of specific indicators. Nor are all indicators relevant to the agricultural situation in all countries, but in certain cases others are highly relevant for all countries (for example, indicators on water quality). It should be noted that data for all indicators proposed are national averages, which often encompass wide variations within a country.

Third, as in most other domains of measurement, indicators are often proxies and context-specific and need to be read in conjunction with other indicators on the list.

Fourth, the proposed indicators related to policy tools refer only to market-based instruments and do not include indicators for regulatory instruments. Construction of indicators for regulations is complicated due to the fact that information is often of a qualitative nature and is not easy to compare across countries. Consideration should be given to how indicators on economic instruments can be complemented by indicators on environmental regulation so as to balance international comparisons of policy responses.

Finally, gaps exist and some of the selected indicators are not measurable at present and merit further development. Among the areas identified as having the largest gaps were indicators concerning green innovation and investment in agriculture, the natural asset base, and the environmental quality of life.

Further improvements in monitoring the progress of green growth in agriculture will largely depend on follow-up work currently underway or planned in the context of the OECD *Green Growth Measurement* agenda, on the finalisation and implementation of the SEEA, and other relevant work, such as the World Bank's Wealth Accounting and Valuation of Ecosystem Services (WAVES) project.

The OECD, UNEP, the World Bank and the Global Green Growth Institute (GGGI) are working together via the Green Growth Knowledge Platform (GGKP) to help countries advance on the measurement, design and implementation of green growth policies. Where possible and meaningful, the indicators proposed by the various international agencies are being harmonised. A first step towards a common internationally-agreed approach was made in April 2013 with the publication of *Moving towards a Common Approach on Green Growth Indicators*, prepared jointly by the GGKP member organisations (GGKP, 2013). This common approach is based on the OECD Green Growth measurement framework.

The SEEA is a crucial ingredient of the measurement agenda as it provides an overarching, consistent statistical framework for compiling and presenting economic and environmental data (UN 2014). It constitutes an accounting framework that will ensure consistent basic data for environmental and economic variables. Furthermore, it provides an integrated framework for the compilation of statistics on the various aspects of wider concepts. Its implementation is expected to maximise international comparability and consistency and it will become the primary framework from which green growth indicators will be derived.

Note

1. A similar exercise was performed jointly by the OECD and the International Energy Agency (IEA) for the energy sector, where a set of indicators was proposed (OECD, 2011c).

Bibliography

European Commission (EC) (2011), *Economic Analysis of Resource Efficiency Policies: Final Report*, DG Environment, Brussels.

Green Growth Knowledge Platform (GGKP) (2013), *Moving towards a Common Approach on Green Growth Indicators, Green Growth Knowledge Platform Scoping Paper*, April, www.oecd.org/greengrowth/GGKP%20Moving%20towards%20a%20Common%20Approach%20on%20Green%20Growth%20Indicators%5B1%5D.pdf.

OECD (2014), *Green Growth Indicators 2014*, OECD Green Growth Studies, OECD Publishing, Paris, doi: http://dx.doi.org/10.1787/9789264202030-en.

OECD (2013a), *Policy Instruments to Support Green Growth in Agriculture; A Synthesis of Country Experiences,* OECD Publishing, Paris, http://dx.doi.org/10.1787/9789264203525-en

OECD (2013b), *OECD Compendium of Agri-environmental Indicators,* OECD Publishing, Paris, doi: http://dx.doi.org/10.1787/9789264186217-en.

OECD (2012), *Evaluation of Agri-Environmental Policies: Selected Methodological Issues and Case Studies*, OECD publishing, Paris, doi: http://dx.doi.org/10.1787/9789264179332-en.

OECD (2011a), *Towards Green Growth,* OECD Green Growth Studies, OECD Publishing, Paris, http://dx.doi.org/10.1787/9789264111318-en.

OECD (2011b), *Towards Green Growth: Monitoring Progress: OECD Indicators*, OECD Green Growth Studies, OECD Publishing, Paris, doi: http://dx.doi.org/10.1787/9789264111356-en.

OECD (2011c), *OECD Green Growth Studies – Energy*, OECD Publishing, Paris, doi: http://dx.doi.org/10.1787/9789264115118-en.

OECD (2009), *Methods to Monitor and Evaluate the Impacts of Agricultural Policies on Rural Development*, OECD report, Paris, http://www.oecd.org/agriculture/44559121.pdf.

United Nations (UN) (2014), *System of Environmental Economic Accounting – Central Framework*, European Commission, FAO, IMF, OECD, UN, the World Bank, United Nations, New York. http://unstats.un.org/unsd/envaccounting/seeaRev/SEEA_CF_Final_en.pdf.

United Nations Environment Programme (UNEP) (2012a), *Measuring Progress Towards an Inclusive Green Economy*, UNEP, Nairobi.

UNEP (2012b), *Green Economy: Metrics and Indicators*, Briefing Paper, UNEP DTIE, Geneva.

UNEP (2012c), *Measuring Water Use in a Green Economy, A report of the Working Group on Water Efficiency to the International resource Panel*, Geneva.

World Bank (2012), *Inclusive Growth: The Pathway to Sustainable Development*, World Bank, Washington, D.C.

Chapter 2

Contextual indicators for agricultural growth

Interpretation and assessment of green growth indicators for agriculture need to take into account the socio-economic circumstances of individual countries. This chapter provides information on the economic context and key characteristics of agricultural growth, particularly with regard to productivity, trade and commodity prices.

The statistical data for Israel are supplied by and under the responsibility of the relevant Israeli authorities. The use of such data by the OECD is without prejudice to the status of the Golan Heights, East Jerusalem and Israeli settlements in the West Bank under the terms of international law.

Indicators for agricultural growth provide information on the socio-economic context and key characteristics of such growth. There are several relevant indicators, including: the relative importance of the sector in the economy in terms of GDP, employment and trade; the socio-economic structure of the sector (education levels, age); commodity prices; type of production (e.g. crops, livestock) and type of productivity (multifactorial, partial, yields).

For the purpose of this study, the indicators listed in **Table 2.1** provide information on the economic performance of the agricultural sector, particularly with regard to agricultural economic growth and productivity, trade and commodity prices. Indicators reflecting the socio-economic characteristics of this sector, such as education and age structure, are included under policy responses and opportunities group of indicators.

Table 2.1. Measuring the economic performance of agriculture

Theme	Indicator
Economic growth	Growth of total agricultural production (volume)
Productivity	Total factor productivity
Trade	Relative importance of agricultural trade
Commodity prices	Trends in real international commodity prices
	Supplementary indicators
	Share of agricultural GDP in total
	Share of agricultural employment in total
	Growth of crop production (volume)
	Growth of livestock production (volume)
	Agricultural labour productivity growth rates
	Agricultural capital productivity growth rates
	Growth rates in yields

Measurability

Data on economic indicators are available across a wide range of countries and over time. Data on agricultural Gross Domestic Product (GDP) and employment, for example, are published by the World Bank and EUROSTAT, while data on international commodity prices are published by the IMF and FAO. Data on agricultural production volume are indices published by FAO. They show the relative level of the aggregate volume of agricultural production for each year in comparison with the base period 1999-2001.

Data on total factor productivity (TFP) and trade are published by OECD. Data on TFP are available for 20 countries from 1990 and are updated regularly. However, further efforts are needed to improve the availability and comparability of TFP by sector. For agriculture, the estimates on TFP also include hunting, forestry and fisheries. Moreover, due to the lack of data on investment by industry and by asset – a major requirement to obtain capital services series as a measure for capital input in the OECD productivity at the total economy level – the estimates of TFP at the sectoral level is computed using net capital stocks.

Although a country's GDP (total and sectoral) is the most widely-used measure of economic growth, GDP and other standard economic indicators measure only the monetary value of goods and services produced in an economy in a given time period. It does not account for the depreciation of the produced asset as it affects the depletion of natural assets nor does it measure well-being (see, for example, Arrow et al., 2012; Nordhaus, 1974; Solow, 1974; and the report by the international Commission on *Measurement of Economic Performance* (Stiglitz, Sen and Fittousi, 2011).

Main trends

Relative importance of the sector

In most OECD countries, the direct economic contribution of the primary agricultural sector to the overall economy to GDP and employment creation is small (**Figure 2.1**). On average, agriculture in the OECD area accounts for around 2.6% of GDP and 5% of total employment. Nevertheless, the relative importance of agricultural trade has increased (**Figure 2.2**). The indicator proposed here aims to capture the exposure of a country's agricultural sector to international competition.

Figure 2.1. Agriculture's contribution to the economy, 2010 or latest

Share in GDP

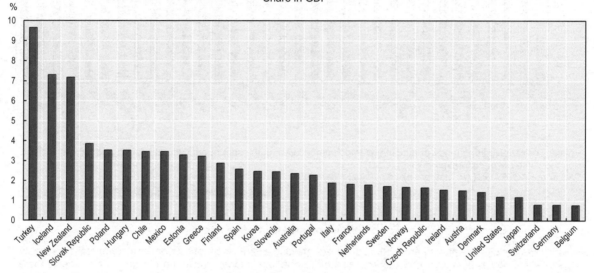

Share in employment

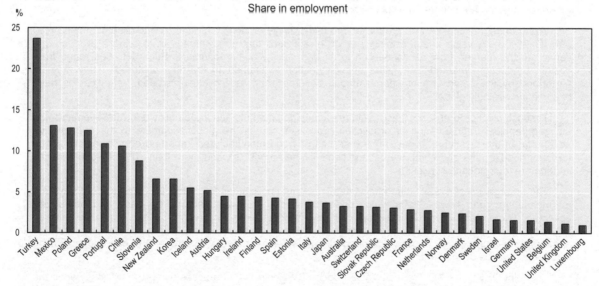

Note: GDP data for 2010 refer to the year 2009 for Iceland. Employment data for 2010 refer to the year 2009 for Australia, Israel and New Zealand.
Source: World Bank, *World Development Indicators (database)* http://data.worldbank.org/data-catalog/world-development-indicators.

StatLink ᴍˢᴾ http://dx.doi.org/10.1787/888933144460

Figure 2.2. Importance of agricultural trade in OECD countries, 2010

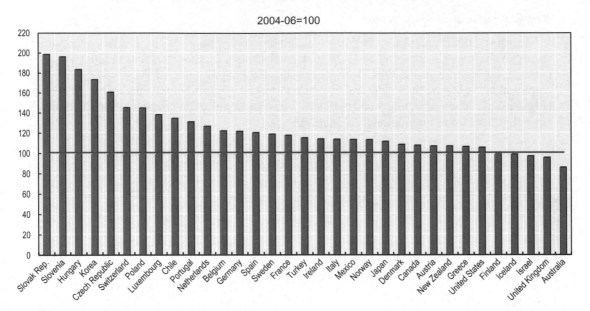

2004-06=100

Note: The relative importance of agricultural trade is measured as the sum of agricultural imports and exports divided by the value of agricultural production (USD).
Source: FAO, FAOSTAT (database), http://faostat.fao.org/.

StatLink http://dx.doi.org/10.1787/888933144477

Box 2.1. Measuring trade in value added

With the globalisation of production, there is a growing awareness that conventional trade statistics may give a misleading perspective of the importance of trade to economic growth and income. This reflects the fact that trade flows are measured gross and that the value of products that cross borders several times for further processing are counted multiple times.

World trade, investment and production are increasingly organised around global value chains (GVCs) (OECD, 2013a). A value chain is the full range of activities that firms engage in to bring a product or a service to the market, from its conception to its end use by final consumers. Such activities range from design, production, marketing, logistics and distribution to support to the final customer. They may be performed by the same firm or shared among several firms. As they have spread, value chains have become increasingly global.

Technological progress, cost, access to resources and markets and trade policy reforms have facilitated the geographical fragmentation of production processes across the globe according to the comparative advantage of the locations. Today, more than half of world manufactured imports are intermediate goods (primary goods, parts and components, and semi-finished products), and more than 70% of world services imports are intermediate services.

The emergence of global value chains has important implications for policy, including trade policy, and for measuring trade flows. Global value chains challenge the way statistics on trade and output are collected. Trade statistics in particular are collected in gross terms and record several times the value of intermediate inputs traded along the value chain. As a consequence, the country of the final producer appears as capturing most of the value of goods and services traded, while the role of countries providing inputs upstream is overlooked.

The joint OECD – WTO Trade in Value-Added (TiVA) initiative addresses this issue by considering the value added by each country in the production of goods and services that are consumed worldwide. TiVA indicators are designed to better inform policy makers by providing new insights into the commercial relations between nations.

Source: OECD (2014), *Measuring Trade in Value Added: An OECD-WTO joint initiative*, www.oecd.org/sti/ind/measuringtradeinvalue-addedanoecd-wtojointinitiative.htm

---

In addition, as world trade, investment and production are increasingly structured around so-called "global value chains" (GVCs) where the different stages of the production process are located across different countries, it is useful to measure the importance of GVCs in agriculture (**Box 2.1**). The GVC perspective links the primary agricultural sector to downstream activities ("agri-food business") and thus the indicators proposed cover both agriculture, and the food and beverage sectors. The indicators proposed are: 1) the participation index, which captures the import content of exports; and 2) the "distance" to final demand, which measures the position of the country in the agro-food global value chain.[1]

Figure 2.3. Participation and position in GVCs for agriculture and food products, 2009

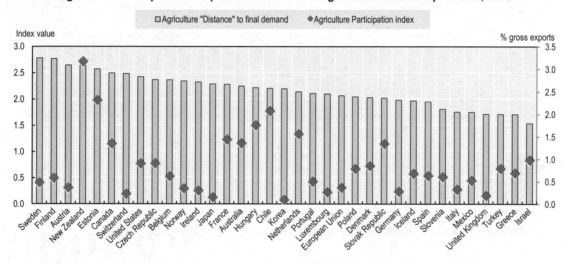

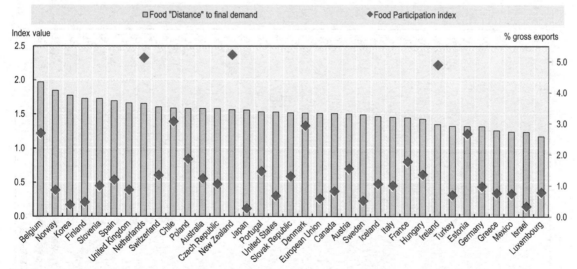

Source: OECD/WTO (2013), *OECD-WTO: Statistics on Trade in Value Added*, (database). http://stats.oecd.org/index.aspx?queryid=47807.

StatLink ⟐ http://dx.doi.org/10.1787/10.1787/888933144485

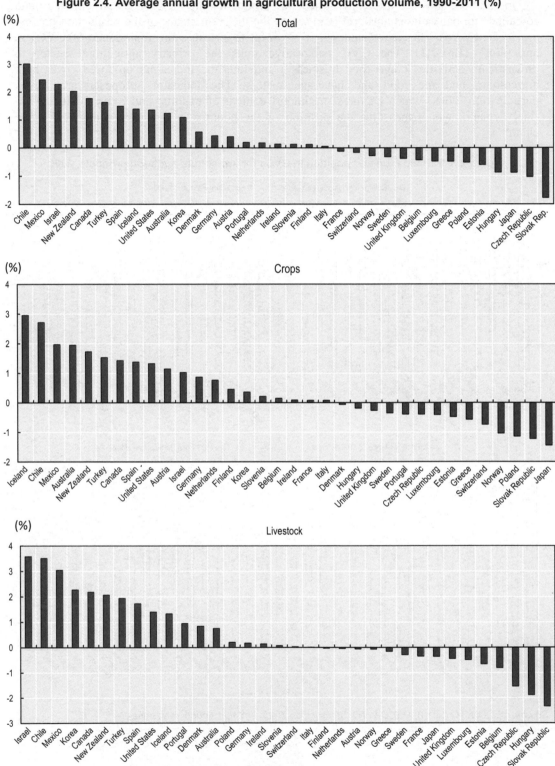

Figure 2.4. Average annual growth in agricultural production volume, 1990-2011 (%)

Note: The least-squares growth rate, r, is estimated by fitting a linear regression trend line to the logarithmic annual values of the variable in the relevant period, as follows: Ln(xt) = a + r * t and is calculated as [exp(r) – 1].
Source: OECD Secretariat calculations based on FAO, FAOSTAT (database), http://faostat.fao.org/.

StatLink ⟨⟩ http://dx.doi.org/10.1787/10.1787/888933144494

New Zealand, Estonia and Chile are the three economies whose global value chain represents the highest percentage of agricultural exports; in the food products value chain, the global value chain of New Zealand, the Netherlands and Ireland represents the highest percentage of exports (**Figure 2.3**). In terms of patterns of specialisation, Sweden, Finland and Austria have the highest index of upstream activities in agriculture, and Belgium, Norway, Finland, the Netherlands and the United Kingdom have the highest index in terms of food products.

Agricultural production

Agricultural production has increased for most OECD countries over the last two decades (**Figure 2.4**). Production growth was higher than 2% per year for Chile, Israel and Mexico, while several OECD countries experienced negative growth, albeit very small (e.g. less than 1% per annum). While in some countries growth in total agricultural production resulted from growth in the production of both crops and livestock (e.g. Australia, Canada, Chile, New Zealand, Spain and the United States), in others either production of crops or livestock has declined (e.g. Austria, Belgium, Denmark).

Agricultural production is projected to expand over the next decade, but at a slower rate than in the preceding one (2003-12), down from 2.1% to 1.5% per annum (OECD, 2013b), with significant international differences across countries and commodities. This slower growth is expected to be exhibited by all crop sectors and livestock production. Rising costs, growing resource constraints and increasing environmental pressure are the main factors explaining these trends.

Productivity

Agricultural growth can arise from a number of sources: changes in real (adjusted for inflation) prices (or the "terms of trade" effect), increased agricultural land and greater yields. Higher real prices or improved terms of trade increase the value of the same quantity of output, while area and yield growth result in a larger quantity of output (real output growth). Yield growth itself can occur either from intensifying the use of existing technology (for example, using more fertiliser or labour per hectare) or from greater efficiency in overall input use (getting more output from a given level of inputs).

Greater efficiency in overall input use is known as growth in total factor (input) productivity or multi-factor productivity. TFP is often associated with new technology or farming practices (innovation). TFP will also increase if resources are shifted from producing lower valued outputs to higher valued outputs. It is widely agreed that increased productivity, arising from innovation and changes in technology, is the main contributor to economic growth in OECD agriculture.

TFP of agriculture (including forestry, hunting and fishing) has grown at a slower rate in the 2000s relative to the 1990s in most OECD countries for which data are available (**Figure 2.5**). Austria, Germany, the Netherlands, Norway and Spain are the exceptions.

Single factor productivity measures, such as productivity of labour, capital and land (yields), are often used because the underlying data are more easily available. While useful, such measures can be misleading as they provide only a partial view of productivity. For example, partial measures by considering output relative to only one input ignore the potential for new technology or efficiency improvements to raise productivity by saving or shifting resources to produce more highly valued outputs. In addition, partial measures do not distinguish between the effects of a more intensive use of existing technology and the effects of adopting new technology.

For these reasons, single factor productivity indicators are also provided as supplementary indicators (**Figures 2.6**, **2.7** and **2.8**). These data suggest that over the last two decades the highest increase in agricultural labour productivity was found in Slovenia, Korea and the Slovak Republic. Mexico, Germany and New Zealand registered the highest increase in investment productivity (agricultural production divided by net capital stock in agriculture), while the highest increase in yield was observed in Estonia and Portugal.

Figure 2.5. Total factor productivity (TFP) of agriculture, annual growth rates (%)

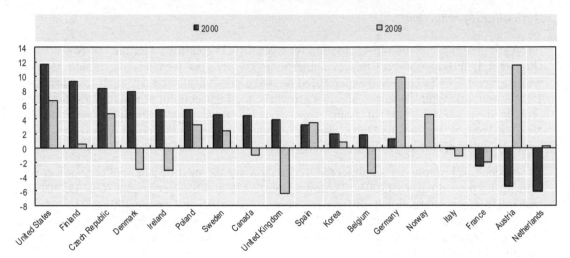

Note: Includes forestry, hunting and fishing. Data for 2009 refer to the year 2008 for Austria, the Czech Republic, Ireland the United Kingdom; to the year 2007 for Canada, France and Norway; and to the year 2006 for Korea and Poland.

Source: OECD (2014), "Productivity by industry", *OECD Productivity Statistics* (database). http://doi/10.1787/pdtvy-data-en.

StatLink ᕬᔆᕒ *http://dx.doi.org/10.1787/888933144503*

Figure 2.6. Cereal yield growth rates, 1990-2011 (%)

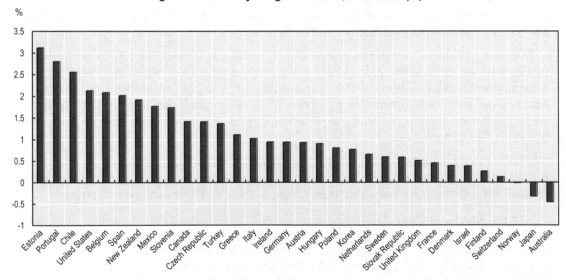

Source: FAO, *FAOSTAT* (database), http://faostat.fao.org/.

StatLink ᕬᔆᕒ *http://dx.doi.org/10.1787/10.1787/888933144519*

Figure 2.7. Agricultural labour productivity growth rates, 1990-2010 (%)

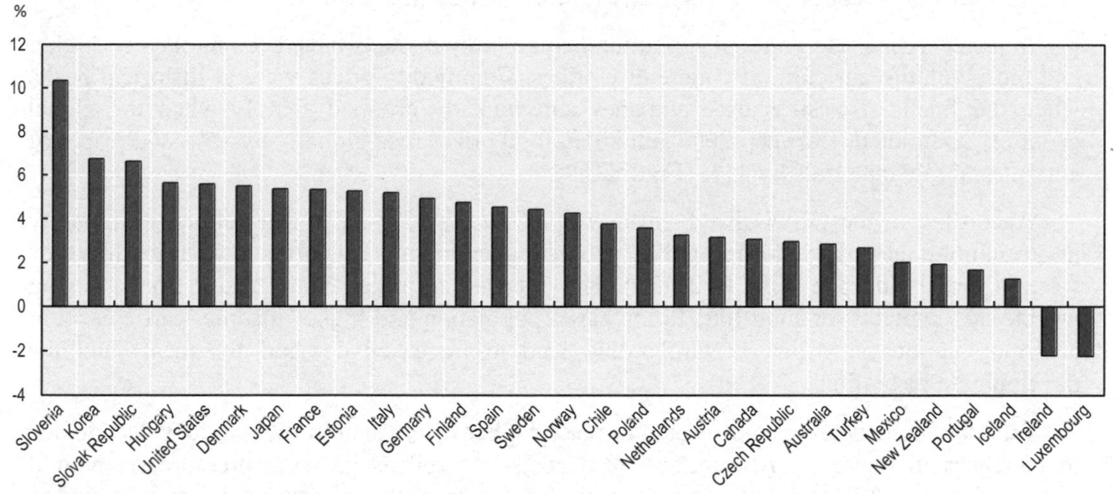

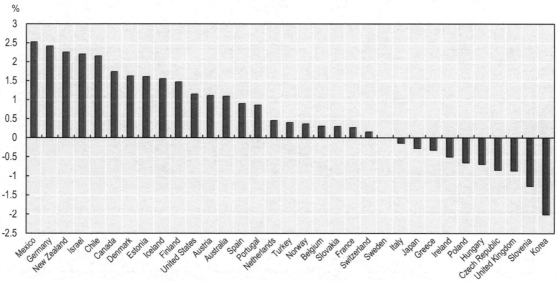

Note: Agricultural labour productivity is defined as agriculture value added per worker (constant USD 2000).

Source: The World Bank, *World Development Indicators (database)*, http://data.worldbank.org/data-catalog/world-development-indicators.

StatLink http://dx.doi.org/10.1787/888933144526

Figure 2.8. Agricultural investment productivity growth, 1990-2007 (1990=100)

Note: Investment productivity is defined as agricultural production at constant 2004-06 prices (million USD) divided by net capital stock in agriculture at constant 2005 prices (million USD).

Source: FAO, *FAOSTAT* (database), http://faostat.fao.org/.

StatLink http://dx.doi.org/10.1787/888933144534

Commodity prices

Long-term trends in commodity prices in real terms provide signals about the scarcity or abundance of natural resources and affect economic behaviour. Commodity price increases could provide incentives for farmers to boost production which in turn may increase the pressure on the environment, depending on the farming practices, systems and technologies adopted, as well as the environmental sensitivity of the location where production increases occur. Strong volatile price movements, on the other hand, tend to send unreliable signals that may or may not be conducive to more environmentally-benign growth.

In recent years, international agricultural commodity markets have been marked by higher and more volatile agricultural commodity prices. Commodity prices were at historical peaks when the financial crisis started and they subsequently dropped sharply when the global economy contracted. Between 2009 and 2010, food prices rose globally by 15% and prices of agricultural raw materials by 31% (**Figure 2.9**).

According to the OECD-FAO *Agricultural Outlook 2013-2022*, agricultural commodity prices in nominal and real terms are likely to be higher and more volatile on average than they were in the last decade (OECD, 2013b). This increase in prices would result from growing world-wide demand for food (due to increased population and higher income, particularly in emerging countries, which in turn would lead to increased demand for meat) and the development of biofuels.

Production costs are also projected to reach higher levels than in the previous decade due to increases in energy, fertilisers and feed costs, as well as growing pressure on natural resources, especially land and water. Over the next decade, the crude oil price is projected to rise, which may translate into higher farm input prices (e.g. fertilisers, energy to pump water, pesticides). Overall, with the increase in output prices on the one hand, and rising farm input prices on the other, the expected environmental outcomes could be ambiguous depending on the intensity and location of production effects.

Figure 2.9. Evolution of primary commodity prices
2005=100

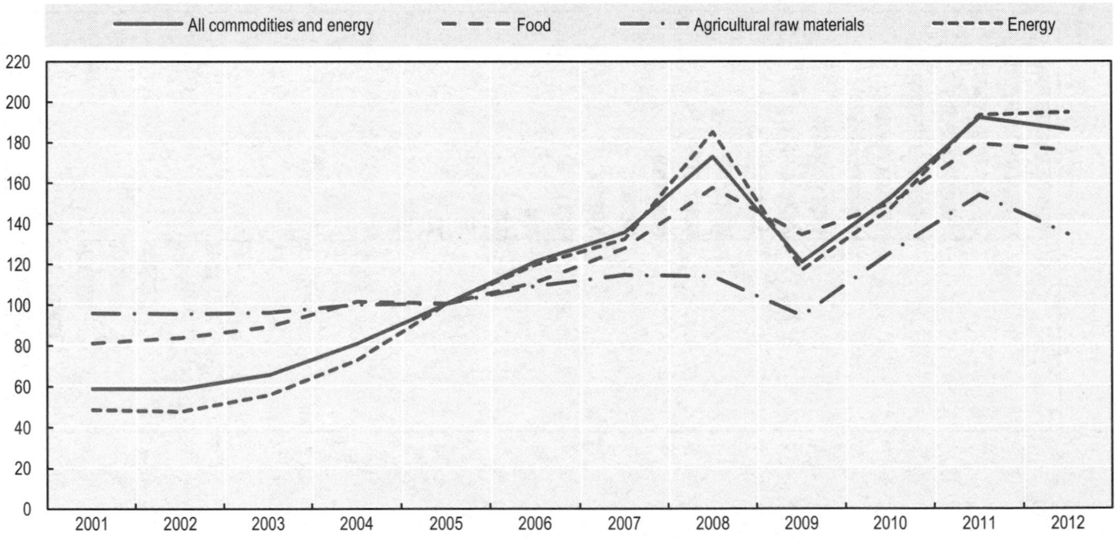

Source: International Monetary Fund (2013), *IMF Primary Commodity Prices* (database), http://www.imf.org/external/np/res/commod/index.aspx.

StatLink ᵐˢᵖ http://dx.doi.org/10.1787/888933144540

Note

1. The distance to final demand measures the number of stages between production and final demand and is an indicator of "upstreamness" in a global value chain. Longer distances indicate a specialisation in producing inputs closer to the start of the value chain, which includes higher-value activities, such as R&D. The participation index is calculated as the sum of: 1) the share of foreign inputs in overall exports, and 2) the share of gross exports that are used as inputs in other countries' exports.

Bibliography

Arrow, K.J., P. Dasgupta, L.H. Goulder, K.J. Mumford, and K. Oleson (2012), "Sustainability and the measurement of wealth", *Environment and Development Economics*, Vol. 17, No. 3.

FAO, *FAOSTAT* (database), FAO, Rome, http://faostat.fao.org/.

Nordhaus, W.D. (1974), "Resources as a Constraint on Growth", *American Economic Review*, Vol. 64, No. 2.

International Monetary Fund (2013), IMF Primary Commodity Prices (database), http://www.imf.org/external/np/res/commod/index.aspx.

OECD (2014a), *Measuring Trade in Value Added: An OECD-WTO joint initiative*, www.oecd.org/sti/ind/measuringtradeinvalue-addedanoecd-wtojoint initiative.htm.

OECD (2014b), "GDP per capita and productivity levels", *OECD Productivity Statistics* (database), doi: http://dx.doi.org/10.1787/data-00686-en.

OECD (2013a), *Interconnected Economies: Benefiting from Global Value Chains*, OECD Publishing, Paris, doi: http://dx.doi.org/10.787/9789264189560-en.

OECD (2013b), *OECD/FAO Agricultural Outlook 2013-22*, OECD Publishing, Paris, doi: http://dx.doi.org/10.1787/agr_outlook-2013-en.

OECD/FAO (2013b), *OECD-FAO Agricultural Outlook 2013*, OECD Publishing, Paris doi: http://dx.doi.org/10.1787/agr_outlook-2013-en.

Solow, R.M. (1974), "The Economics of Resources or the Resources of Economics", *American Economic Review, Papers and Proceedings*, Vol. 64.

Stiglitz, J., A. Sen and J.P. Fittousi (2011), *Report by the Commission on Measurement of Economic Performance*, www.stiglitz-sen-fitoussi.fr/en/index.htm.

World Bank, *World Development Indicators (database)*, http://data.worldbank.org/data-catalog/world-development-indicators.

Chapter 3

Monitoring the environmental efficiency and natural resource productivity of agriculture

Tracking trends in decoupling inputs to production from economic growth is an important issue for monitoring progress towards green growth. Indicators included in this chapter attempt to capture the extent to which economic growth is becoming greener, that is, low-carbon and resource-efficient. The indicators presented pertain to: i) carbon and energy productivity, which characterises, among other things, interactions with the climate system and the global carbon cycle as well as the environmental and economic efficiency with which energy resources are used in agricultural production; ii) resource productivity, which characterises the environmental and economic efficiency with which natural resources such as water and nutrients are used in production; and iii) environmentally adjusted total factor productivity in order to give a more complete picture of the productivity of an economy by accounting for inputs from natural resources and for the generation of pollution.

The statistical data for Israel are supplied by and under the responsibility of the relevant Israeli authorities. The use of such data by the OECD is without prejudice to the status of the Golan Heights, East Jerusalem and Israeli settlements in the West Bank under the terms of international law.

Indicators that monitor the environmental efficiency and natural resource productivity of agriculture attempt to track the extent to which economic growth is becoming greener (low-carbon and resource-efficient). Tracking trends in the decoupling of inputs to production from economic growth is thus an important focus for monitoring. To achieve this, indicators that focus on environment-related "productivity," or its inverse, "intensity," should be used. Such indicators include those that monitor the productivity of natural resources and materials used in agricultural production (**Box 3.1**).

Improvements in resource productivity (i.e. reducing the amount of resources used per unit of economic output) imply that less resources per unit of economic activity (e.g. agricultural GDP) will be required in the future. Monitoring natural resource and environmental productivity for agriculture is important because of the sector's significant role in using natural resources, making the productivity of soil and water resources of utmost importance.

Box 3.1. The resource productivity concept

Resource productivity refers to the effectiveness with which an economy or a production process is using natural resources. It should ideally encompass all natural resources and ecosystem inputs that are used as factors of production in the economy. This term, however, is often used as a synonym for material productivity. Productivity measurement and analysis of natural resource and material flows complement the traditional indicators of capital, land and labour productivity. Used in parallel, these three types of productivity indicators afford a much deeper understanding of total factor productivity. While there is no disagreement on this general notion, a look at the productivity literature and its various applications reveals there is no single purpose or indicator to measure productivity. Productivity can be defined with respect to:

- The economic-physical efficiency (i.e. the value of output or value added generated per unit of resource inputs used).

- The physical or technical efficiency (i.e. the amount of resources input required to produce a unit of output, both expressed in physical terms, such as land for the production of cereals). The focus is on maximising the output with a given set of inputs and a given technology or on minimising the inputs for a given output.

- The economic efficiency (i.e. the money value of outputs relative to the money value of inputs). The focus is on minimising resource input costs.

The OECD places "resource productivity" within a welfare perspective. It is understood to contain both a quantitative dimension (e.g. the quantity of output produced with a given input of natural resources) and a qualitative dimension (e.g. the environmental impacts per unit of output produced with a given natural resource input).

Improving resource productivity is often assumed to lead to a parallel reduction in environmental impact to help avert the possibility of resource scarcity and environmental degradation. However, unless such improvements outweigh economic growth, there is a risk that the associated negative environmental impacts might increase. Protecting and managing the natural resource base cannot, therefore, rely on improvements in resource productivity alone; it will also be necessary to de-link economic growth from environmental pressures (**Box 3.2**). While productivity indicators and their inverse – decoupling trends – show whether production has become *greener* in *relative* terms, they do not show whether environmental pressure has also diminished in *absolute* terms. From an environmental perspective it is useful to also monitor the presence of absolute decoupling.

Box 3.2. Decoupling concepts

De-linking – commonly called decoupling – environmental impacts from economic growth is a core goal of the OECD Green Growth Strategy. The concept of resource decoupling was officially endorsed by OECD Environment Ministers in 2001 and is considered a main objective in the Environmental Strategy for the First Decade of the 21st Century (www.oecd.org/dataoecd/33/40/1863539.pdf). The OECD was mandated to undertake the task of developing a set of indicators to measure progress across the three dimensions of sustainable development. They include indicators to measure the decoupling of economic growth from environmental degradation that might also be used in conjunction with other indicators in the OECD's economic, social, and environmental peer review processes (OECD, 2002).

There are two types of decoupling, commonly referred to as *absolute* and *relative* decoupling. Decoupling is said to be relative when the relevant environmental parameter (e.g. resources used, or a measure of environmental impact) is increasing at a slower rate than the relevant economic variable (e.g. GDP); that is, the economy is growing faster than resource use, while the absolute quantity of the resource input is still increasing (i.e. the elasticity is positive, but less than unity). Such relative decoupling appears to be fairly common. Decoupling is said to be absolute when the economic variable is growing, while the environmental variable is stable or decreasing.

The decoupling concept, however, does not automatically capture the environmental impacts associated with economic growth. The relationship between resource use, environmental pressures and environmental impacts is complex. Taking resource-use as a proxy for environmental impacts can be misleading: first, the entire life-cycle of resources, from their extraction, through their use in the production of goods and services and subsequent use phase, to the waste phase, gives rise to environmental impacts; second, any given natural resource material can take numerous different pathways through the economy, which can change with time (as a result of technical or social developments, for example); third, differences in regional conditions and use patterns also need to be considered. Furthermore, the extent of the environmental impact varies according to the resources used.

For these reasons, two dimensions of decoupling as applied to green growth are distinguished in the literature: *resource* decoupling and *impact* decoupling (**Figure 3.1**). The former addresses the link between economic growth versus resource use, while the latter refers to the link between economic growth versus environmental impact (i.e. increasing economic output while reducing negative environmental impacts) (UNEP, 2011). In terms of methodology and data collection, impact decoupling is usually very demanding at the aggregate level (national or sectoral) as many environmental impacts, which may have quite different trends, need to be considered, and the weighting procedures necessary for aggregating the impacts might be seen as subjective. Moreover, a negative relation between these two concepts of decoupling might occur, as reducing environmental impact does not necessarily have a mitigating impact on resource scarcity or production costs, and may even increase them. There is a significant volume of theoretical and empirical studies which examines whether or not increased efficiency leads to environmental improvements; the so-called "rebound effect" or Jevons' paradox. In general, the magnitude of the rebound effect is driven by the degree of substitution between factors of production (e.g. energy, capital) (Sorrell, 2009; Sorrell, Dimitropoulos and Sommerville, 2009).

Figure 3.1. Stylised representation of resource and impact decoupling

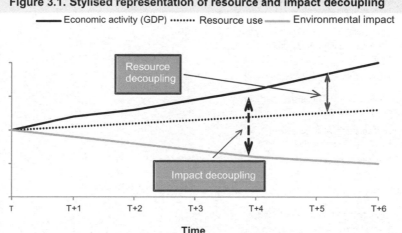

Moreover, productivity or intensity indicators need to be gauged in the specific (country) context regarding the country's level of development or endowment of natural assets. Specific indicators selected for this group should track the productivity of those natural resources that are most important to domestic agricultural production. Thus, specific indicators selected in this group will vary across countries. For example, indicators related to the intensity of water use in agriculture may be considered irrelevant by those countries possessing abundant water resources.

Other indicators, however, will be common across countries, in particular those that are global in nature, such as climate change. The atmosphere's capacity to absorb Green House Gases (GHGs) is a global asset and the environmental efficiency of GHG emissions is relevant independent of the country or region in question. Similarly, energy is a critical input into agricultural production and energy productivity is important around the world.

Another limitation of partial indicators is that rising productivity may also be the result of the substitution of natural assets for other inputs (labour, capital, energy) or an overall rise in the efficiency of the production process from improved technology or organisation (i.e. a multi-factor productivity increase). Care must be taken when interpreting partial productivity measures, although the caveats relating to environmental productivity do not differ from those relating, for instance, to traditional partial productivity indicators (e.g. labour productivity). Overall, changes in the natural resource and environmental productivity indicators need to be carefully interpreted. **Table 3.1** presents the proposed indicators in this area.

Table 3.1. Environmental efficiency and natural resource productivity/intensity indicators

Theme	Indicators	Criteria			
		Capturing the nexus between the environment and the economy	Ease of communication for different users and audiences	Reflecting key global environmental issues	Measurability and comparability across countries
Carbon productivity	Agricultural GDP per unit of agricultural GHG emissions	***	***	***	***
	Supplementary indicators				
	Share of agriculture in total GHG emissions	***	***	***	***
	Productivity of GHG emission from agriculture by source (soil, ruminants, manure management)	***	***	***	***
Energy productivity	Agricultural GDP per unit of energy use	***	***	***	***
	Renewable energy produced by agriculture	***	***	***	*
Water use intensity	Irrigation water per irrigated area	***	***	***	*
Nutrient flows and balances	Nutrient (N and P) intensities per area of agricultural land	***	***	***	***
	Nutrient balances in agriculture (N and P) per agricultural output and area	***	***	***	**
	Intensity of commercial fertilisers	***	***	**	***
Material (biomass) productivity		Indicators to be developed			
Multifactor productivity	Environmentally adjusted total factor productivity	***	**	*	*

Carbon productivity

Policy context

Agricultural production not only uses environmental resources as inputs, it also places pressure on the environment by emitting pollutants such as GHGs, therefore contributing to climate change. Agriculture is highly exposed to climate change, which may have an impact on yields, location of production and costs of production and thus with potential risks for food supply, food prices and farm incomes.

The relationship between agriculture and climate change is complex. Agriculture not only contributes to GHGs, but it also provides a carbon sink function under certain management practices. Moreover, agriculture is subject to the impact of climate change. While farming is a source of GHGs, principally methane (CH_4) and nitrous oxide (N_2O), which are part of the primary driving force behind climate change, climate change may also impact on farm production.

Although there are no specific agricultural commitments under the United Nations Framework Convention on Climate Change (UNFCCC) to reduce GHG emissions, many OECD countries are developing agricultural climate change programmes aimed at reducing GHGs, promoting carbon sinks, and making agriculture more resilient to the impact of climate change. A key challenge in relation to agriculture and agricultural GHG emissions is to reduce the overall level and rate of emission release per unit volume of agricultural production.

Monitoring progress

The progress of green growth in agriculture can be assessed against trends in agricultural GHG emissions and the level of decoupling achieved between GHGs and economic growth in agriculture. The proposed indicator relates to the carbon productivity of agriculture defined as the amount of agricultural GDP per unit of carbon equivalents emitted by agriculture.[1] Increasing carbon productivity is key to addressing the twin challenge of mitigating climate change and managing economic growth.

Supplementary indicators might include: i) share of agriculture in total GHG emissions; ii) productivity of agriculture GHG emissions by source: soil denitrification, fermentation of ruminants, manure decomposition and rice cultivation.

GHG productivity is already used as an indicator in OECD and other international organisations that work on green growth. It is widely accepted and easy to interpret.

Measurability

UNFCCC inventories are the main data source. Measurability of indicators is good, as data on GHG emissions are reported annually by Annex I countries to the UNFCCC. The data cover all OECD countries, except Chile, Israel, Korea and Mexico. Emissions are expressed in CO_2-equivalents, as different GHGs have a different global warning potential. The main sources of agricultural GHG emissions are:

- Methane (CH_4) emissions, through enteric fermentation in ruminant animals (cattle, sheep and goats).

- Nitrous oxide (N2O) emissions, produced by soil denitrification.

- CH4 and N2O emissions, from manure decomposition.

These biochemical processes generally depend on climate, agronomic and technological conditions which can affect agricultural soils and manure storage facilities. Methane and nitrous oxide emissions are closely related to livestock production. Since these different

GHG, have different global warming potential, the data are expressed in terms of emissions of CO2-equivalent in order to make them comparable.

Main trends

Primary agriculture in the OECD area accounts, on average, for 8% of total GHGs in the OECD area (**Figure 3.2**). Soil de-nitrification is the main source of GHGs from agriculture (46%), followed by fermentation of ruminants (37%) and manure management (15%) (**Figure 3.3**) Over the period 1990-2010, total OECD agricultural GHG emissions decreased slightly (**Figure 3.4**). Over the same period, agricultural production steadily increased, suggesting that for the OECD area as a whole there has been an improvement in the environmental efficiency of agricultural GHG emissions (**Figure 3.5**). In several cases, absolute decoupling of GHG emissions from agricultural production is observed (**Figure 3.6**). Differences between OECD countries in GHG productivity remain high (**Figure 3.7**). Productivity of GHGs produced by soil de-nitrification, fermentation of ruminants and manure decomposition increased steadily over the 1990-2010 period; productivity of GHGs produced by rice cultivation, on the other hand, exhibited somewhat more variable trends (**Figure 3.8**).

Figure 3.2. Share of agriculture in total GHG emissions, 2008-10 (%)

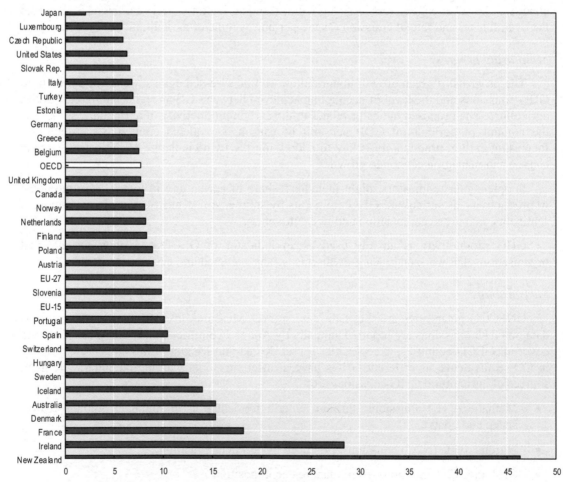

Note: Excluding LULUCF (land use, land use-change and forestry).
Source: UNFCCC *Greenhouse Gas Inventory Data*, http://unfccc.int/ghg_data/items/3800.php.

StatLink ⇒ http://dx.doi.org/10.1787/888933144569

Figure 3.3. GHG emissions from agriculture in the OECD area, by source, 2008-10 (%)

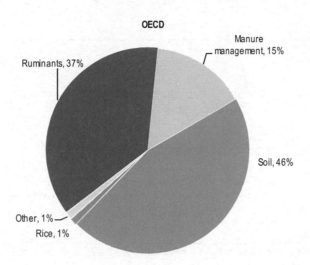

Note: Excluding LULUCF (land use, land use-change and forestry).
Source: UNFCCC *Greenhouse Gas Inventory Data*, http://unfccc.int/ghg_data/items/3800.php.

StatLink ⬛⬛ http://dx.doi.org/10.1787/888933144573

Figure 3.4. Growth rate of total economy and agricultural net GHG emissions

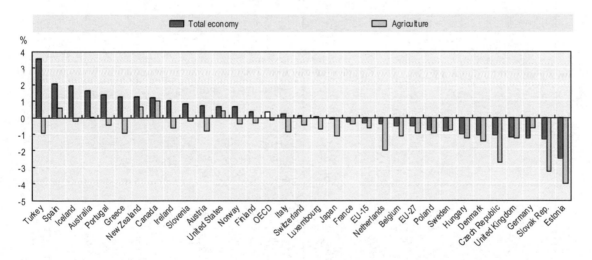

Note: Excluding LULUCF (land use, land use-change and forestry).
Source: UNFCCC *Greenhouse Gas Inventory Data*, http://unfccc.int/ghg_data/items/3800.php.

StatLink ⬛⬛ http://dx.doi.org/10.1787/888933144584

Figure 3.5. GHG emissions, GDP and productivity for agriculture in the OECD area

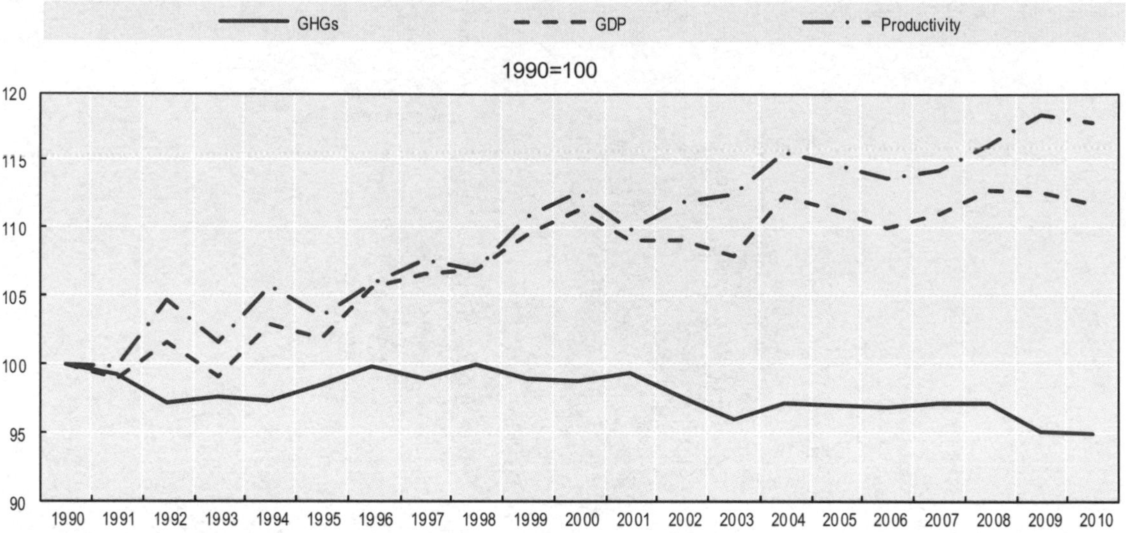

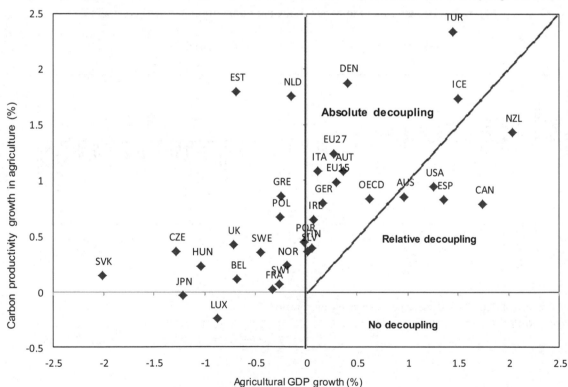

Note: Excluding LULUCF (land use, land use-change and forestry).
Source: UNFCCC *Greenhouse Gas Inventory Data*, http://unfccc.int/ghg_data/items/3800.php; FAO, *FAOSTAT* (database), http://faostat.fao.org/.

StatLink ᠎ http://dx.doi.org/10.1787/888933144592

Figure 3.6. Agricultural economic growth and GHG emissions and relation with decoupling, 1990-2010

Note: Carbon productivity is the agricultural GDP per unit of agricultural GHG emissions.
Source: UNFCCC *Greenhouse Gas Inventory Data*, http://unfccc.int/ghg_data/items/3800.php; FAO, *FAOSTAT* (database), http://faostat.fao.org/.

StatLink ᠎ http://dx.doi.org/10.1787/888933144600

Figure 3.7. Agricultural GHG emissions productivity, 2008-10

OECD = 100

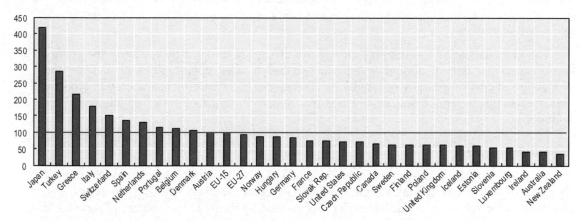

Note: Excluding LULUCF (land use, land use-change and forestry).
Source: UNFCCC *Greenhouse Gas Inventory Data*, http://unfccc.int/ghg_data/items/3800.php.

StatLink ᴍꜱ᠊ᴘ http://dx.doi.org/10.1787/888933144617

Figure 3.8. Agricultural GHG emissions productivity by source in the OECD area

1990=100

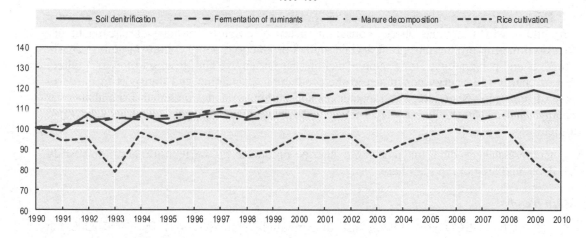

Note: Excluding LULUCF (land use, land use-change and forestry).

Source: UNFCCC *Greenhouse Gas Inventory Data*, http://unfccc.int/ghg_data/items/3800.php; FAO, *FAOSTAT* (database), http://faostat.fao.org/.

StatLink ᴍꜱ᠊ᴘ http://dx.doi.org/10.1787/888933144626

Energy productivity

Policy context

Energy is a key requirement to achieve competitiveness and sustainability in the agricultural sector. The links between agriculture and energy are complex, as agriculture is both a consumer and a producer of energy. Farming consumes energy directly through the use of machinery (e.g. operating machinery and equipment), and the heating of stables and greenhouses, and also consumes energy indirectly, in terms of the energy required to produce fertilisers, pesticides, farm machinery and other inputs. But agriculture is also an important potential source of clean, renewable energy.

Support to agricultural energy use is widespread across OECD countries, mainly through reduced standard rates of fuel tax for on-farm consumption. Support is also common across the OECD area for bioenergy through the provision of a combination of tax incentives and payments for bioenergy production, feedstocks using agricultural raw materials (e.g. maize), and waste (e.g. straw).

The key challenge is to improve energy use efficiency on-farm by lowering the energy consumption per unit of agricultural production and to seek opportunities to increase the production of environmentally neutral biofuel feedstocks (i.e. requiring less energy to produce than the energy generated and having minimal impact in terms of water pollution and air pollution).

Monitoring progress

Progress towards green growth can be assessed against: i) the energy productivity of agriculture (the ratio of agricultural GDP per unit of direct use of energy (solid fuels, oil, gas, electricity, renewables, heat and industrial waste);[2] and ii) trends in the volume of renewable energy produced by agriculture.

These indicators should be studied in conjunction with those concerning GHG emission productivity, R&D and patents related to energy efficiency and renewable energy, energy prices and taxes, and carbon pricing and biofuel support.

Measurability

Data on energy productivity pertain to direct on-farm energy consumption by primary agriculture, which includes energy consumption for: electricity, heating fuel and machinery fuel used in crop production; grain drying, animal production; poultry; transportation of farm products and personal use (for example, heating the farmhouse and driving to town). Indirect use of energy (i.e. energy consumed in the production, packaging and transport to the farm gate of fertilisers, pesticides, farm machinery and buildings) is not included. Data also cover energy used in forestry, which is assumed to be insignificant in most countries relative to agriculture.[3]

Comprehensive data on renewable energy produced by agriculture are not readily available and are not reported here.

Main trends

Across the OECD area, energy use in agriculture increased over the 1990-2000, on average, at a higher rate than agricultural GDP, suggesting that a relative decoupling took place. This trend was reversed in 2000 and onwards, with absolute decoupling as the growth rate in agricultural production outpaced growth in energy productivity, although differences between OECD countries in energy productivity remain high (**Figure 3.9** and **3.10**).

Figure 3.9. Direct on-farm energy productivity, OECD area

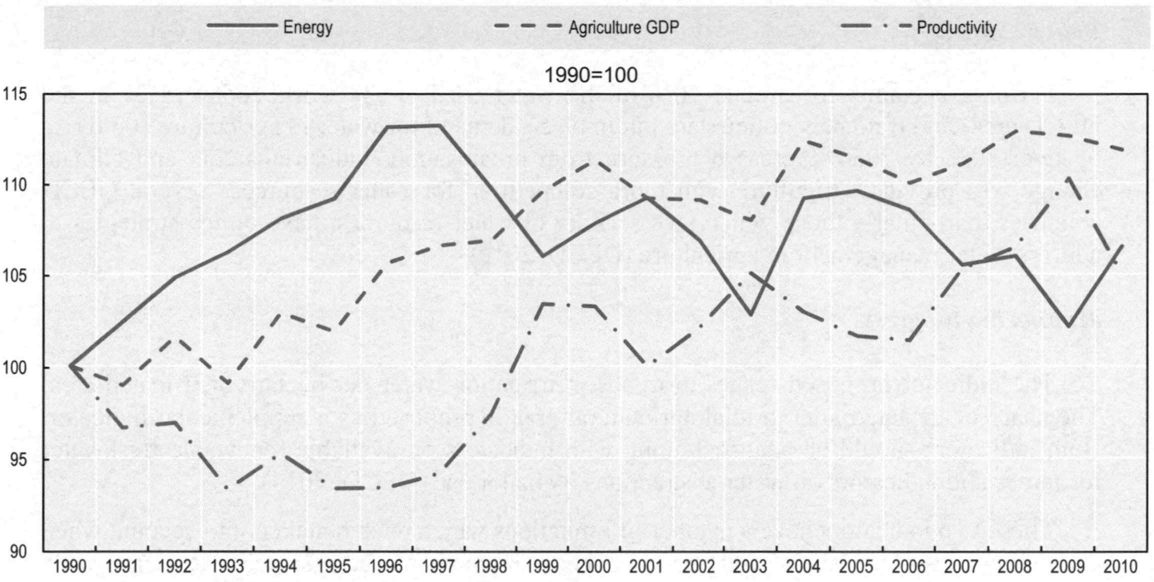

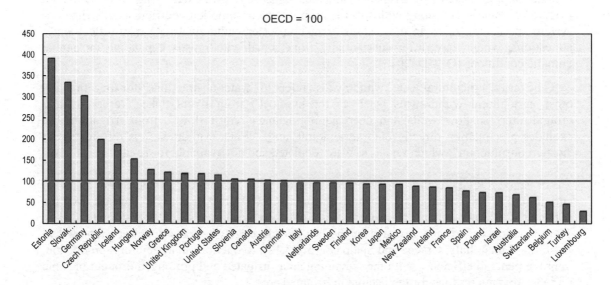

Source: UNFCCC *Greenhouse Gas Inventory Data*, http://unfccc.int/ghg_data/items/3800.php; FAO, *FAOSTAT* (database), http://faostat.fao.org/.

StatLink ⏵ http://dx.doi.org/10.1787/888933144631

Figure 3.10. Direct on-farm energy productivity, 2009-10

OECD = 100

Source: UNFCCC *Greenhouse Gas Inventory Data*, http://unfccc.int/ghg_data/items/3800.php; FAO, *FAOSTAT* (database), http://faostat.fao.org/.

StatLink ⏵ http://dx.doi.org/10.1787/888933144646

Water use intensity

Policy context

Farming accounts for around 70% of the water used in the world today (45% in the OECD area) and if no new policies are put in place, demand for water in agriculture could rise by over 30% by 2050. Increased pressure from urbanisation, industrialisation and climate change will provide agriculture with more competition for water resources. Several OECD countries, particularly those which face scarcity of water resources, have policy strategies to address water management in agriculture (OECD, 2010).

Monitoring progress

The indicator proposed relates to trends in irrigation water per hectare of irrigated area. The share of irrigated area in total agricultural area is proposed as a supplemental indicator. Both indicators should be analysed along with indicators on available renewable freshwater resources and indicators on water abstractions by major use (OECD, 2014).

These two indicators have a number of limitations which must be taken into account when examining absolute levels and trends when comparisons across countries are made (OECD, 2013). In particular, complete and consistent time-series data are available for only a handful of OECD countries (**Figure 3.11**), partly because these data are not usually calculated annually but are derived from five- or even ten-year surveys.

Methods of collecting and calculating the data vary across and within countries and are subject to errors of measurement. Sources of data for irrigation freshwater withdrawals include sample surveys of irrigators, and are sometimes estimated using information on irrigated crop acreages along with specific crop water-consumption coefficients or irrigation-system application rates. In other cases, irrigation water withdrawal data may reflect water allocations, which may differ substantially from actual withdrawals depending on annual climatic conditions (OECD, 2013).

The term "agricultural water withdrawals" refers to "water abstractions" for irrigation and other agricultural withdrawals (such as for livestock) from rivers, lakes, reservoirs and groundwater (shallow wells and deep aquifers), and "return flows" from irrigation, but excludes precipitation directly onto agricultural land. "Water withdrawal" is different from "water consumption", which relates to water depleted and not available for re-use.

In some OECD countries, irrigated agriculture accounts for a significant share of agricultural water withdrawals. Overall, the total OECD area irrigated decreased over the 2000s at -0.4% per annum, compared to a slight increase during the 1990s (OECD, 2013). The reduction in the area irrigated in the last decade largely reflects decreases reported in Australia, Japan, Italy, Greece and Spain (**Figure 3.12**). Reductions in agricultural production, improvements in efficiency with the remaining areas irrigated and prolonged drought in some regions are main reasons for the decline in irrigated area.

Figure 3.11. Agricultural water use intensity versus irrigated area

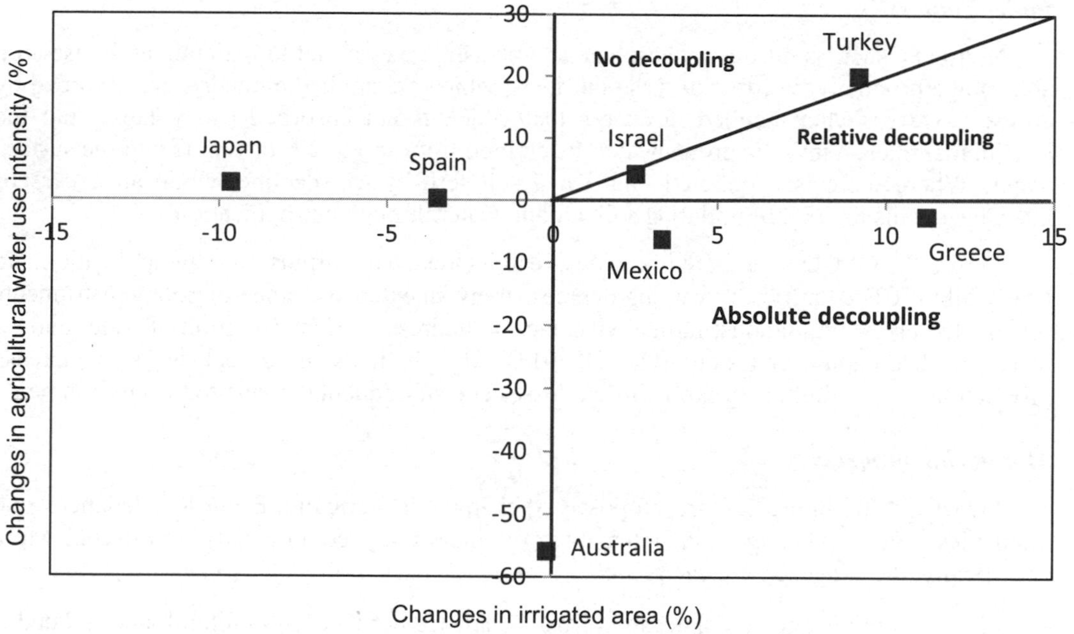

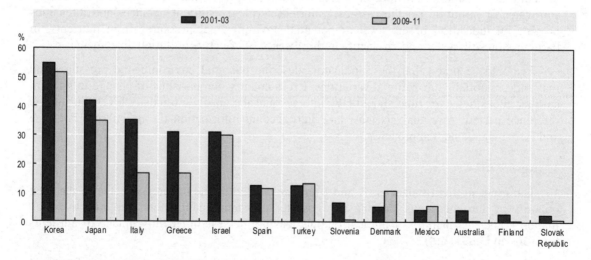

Note: Agricultural water use intensity is defined as irrigation water per irrigated area. Changes refer to the average of 2005-10 and 1990-95.

Source: OECD (2013), "Agri-Environmental Indicators: Environmental Performance of Agriculture 2013", *OECD Agriculture Statistics* (database).
doi: 10.1787/data-00660-en.

StatLink http://dx.doi.org/10.1787/10.1787/888933144654

Figure 3.12. Share of irrigated area

Note: Korea 2007 instead of 2009-11.

Source: World Bank, *World Development Indicators (database)*, http://data.worldbank.org/data-catalog/world-development-indicators.

StatLink http://dx.doi.org/10.1787/888933144666

Nutrient flows and balances

Policy context

Nutrients, such as nitrogen, phosphate and potash, are essential to maintain and raise crop and forage productivity. Most of these nutrients, which are applied annually, are absorbed by crops; however, when applied in excess that which is not absorbed can volatise into the environment, leach into the groundwater, be emitted from soil to air, or runoff into the surface water. Where there is a deficit in nutrients, soil fertility can decline, while an excess of nutrients entails the risk of polluting soil, air and water through eutrophication.

Across the OECD area there is a widespread incidence of surplus nutrient application and nearly all OECD countries, to varying degrees, apply an extensive range of policy instruments (payments, taxes, regulations, farm advice, etc.) to address nutrient pollution of water and air in terms of ammonia emissions (OECD, 2013). The challenge is to seek ways to increase production while minimising farm nutrient losses and subsequent damage to the environment.

Monitoring progress

Two types of indicators are proposed: i) changes in agricultural nutrient balances and intensities and; ii) changes in intensities of inorganic (commercial) fertilisers. More specifically, the proposed indicators are:

- Changes in nitrogen (N) intensity (gross N balance per ha of agricultural land) related to changes in agricultural production.

- Changes in phosphorus (P) intensity (gross P balance per ha of agricultural land) related to changes in agricultural production.

- Changes in commercial fertiliser intensities, calculated by dividing the annual consumption of commercial fertilisers with the area of arable land.

These indicators are proxies of the risk of environmental pressures associated with agricultural production: declining soil fertility (in the case of a nutrient deficit) or the risk of soil/water/air pollution (in the case of a nutrient surplus). Nutrient balances and intensities provide an indication of the level of potential environmental pressures from nutrients, in particular on soil, water and air quality in the absence of effective pollution abatement.

It should be noted that these indicators describe potential environmental pressures and may hide important sub-national variations. Cross-country comparisons of change in nutrient surplus intensities over time should take into account the absolute intensity levels during the reference period. Any analysis must take into account information on agricultural land use and farm management approaches.

Measurability

The gross nutrient balances (N and P) are calculated as the difference between the total quantity of nutrient inputs entering an agricultural system (mainly fertilisers and livestock manure), and the quantity of nutrient outputs leaving the system (mainly uptake of nutrients by crops and grassland).

Nutrient balances are expressed in terms of changes in the physical quantities of nutrient surpluses (deficits) to indicate the trend and level of the potential physical pressure of nutrient surpluses into the environment. The nutrient balance indicator is also expressed in terms of kilogrammes of nutrient surplus (deficit) per hectare of agricultural land per annum to facilitate the comparison between countries of the relative intensity of nutrients in agricultural systems.

Data on nitrogen and phosphorus balances are available for almost all OECD countries from 1990 to 2009 (OECD, 2013). Data on apparent consumption of commercial fertilisers are published by the International Fertiliser Industry Association (IFA) and the FAO.

Main trends

For many OECD countries, nutrient surpluses have been declining over time relative to agricultural output. Overall, OECD agricultural surpluses N and P have been on a continuous downward trend from 1990 to 2009, both in absolute tonnes of nutrients and in terms of nutrient surpluses per hectare of agricultural land. The rate of reduction in nutrient surpluses in the OECD area was more rapid over the 2000s compared to the 1990s, signalling a process of relative decoupling of agricultural production from N- and P-related environmental pressure (**Figure 3.13** and **Figure 3.14**).

A similar picture emerges from the trends in inorganic fertiliser intensities, particularly since 2000; their consumption has been trending downwards, while crop production has been increasing (**Figure 3.15** and **Figure 3.16**).

These developments reflect both improvements in nutrient use efficiency by farmers and slower growth in agricultural output in many countries. The lowering of nutrient surpluses has reduced the risk of environmental pressure on soil, water and air, but sizable variations within and across countries in terms of the intensity and trends of nutrient surpluses indicate various degrees of decoupling.

Figure 3.13. Nutrient balances intensity and agricultural production
OECD area (1990=100)

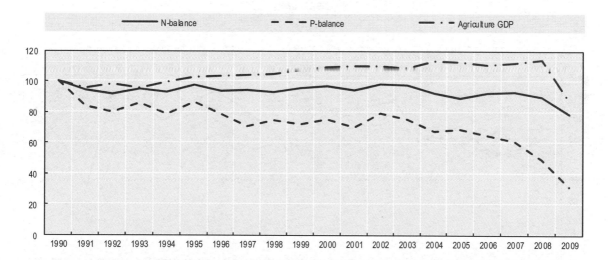

Note: Nutrient balance intensity is defined as the balance (surplus or deficit) of nitrogen and phosphorus per hectare of agricultural land.

Source: OECD (2013), "Agri-Environmental Indicators: Environmental Performance of Agriculture 2013", *OECD Agriculture Statistics* (database).
doi: 10.1787/data-00660-en.

StatLink 🖲 http://dx.doi.org/10.1787/888933144677

Figure 3.14. Nutrient decoupling trends

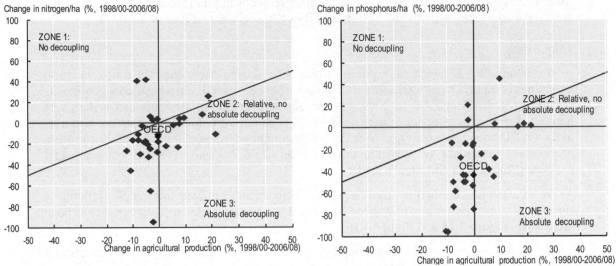

Source: OECD (2014), Decoupling trends: agricultural nutrient balances and agricultural production, in *Green Growth Indicators 2014*, OECD Publishing.
doi: 10.1787/9789264202030-graph25-en.

StatLink ▄▄▄█▄ http://dx.doi.org/10.1787/888933144686

Figure 3.15. Apparent consumption and intensity of inorganic fertilisers, and crop production, OECD area

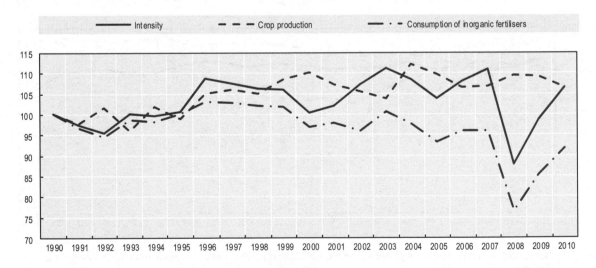

Note: Intensity of inorganic fertiliser is defined as the annual consumption of commercial fertilisers per hectare of arable land.

Source: FAO, *FAOSTAT* (database), http://faostat.fao.org/; International Fertiliser Association (IFA), *IFADATA* (database), http://www.fertilizer.org/Statistics.

StatLink ▄▄▄█▄ http://dx.doi.org/10.1787/888933144690

Figure 3.16. Decoupling trends of inorganic fertilisers

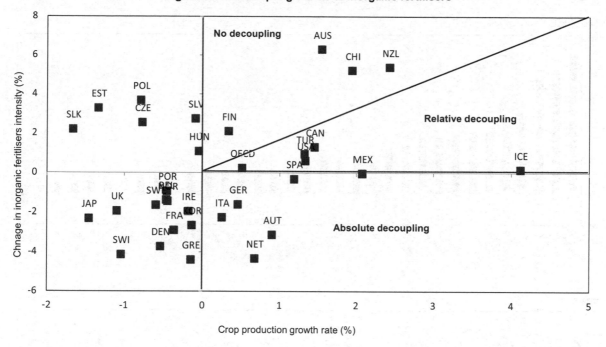

Note: Changes relate to 1990-2010.

Source: FAO, *FAOSTAT* (database), http://faostat.fao.org/; International Fertiliser Association (IFA), *IFADATA* (database), http://www.fertilizer.org/Statistics.

StatLink ᵃᵐˢ⊒ http://dx.doi.org/10.1787/888933144700

Despite the overall improvement in lowering nutrient surpluses, nitrogen and phosphorus intensity levels per hectare of agricultural land remain at very high levels in terms of their potential to cause environmental damage. By 2008-09, around two-thirds of OECD countries had an annual national nitrogen surplus in excess of 40 kgN/ha nitrogen, with Belgium, Israel, Japan, Korea and the Netherlands reporting surpluses in excess of 100 kgN/ha (**Figure 3.17**). Similarly for phosphorus, about one-third of OECD countries had a surplus in excess of 5 kgP/ha, over the same period, with Israel, Japan, Korea, the Netherlands, and Norway, having surpluses in excess of 10 kgP/ha.

Figure 3.17. Nutrient intensities per area of agricultural land, 2008-09 (kg/ha)

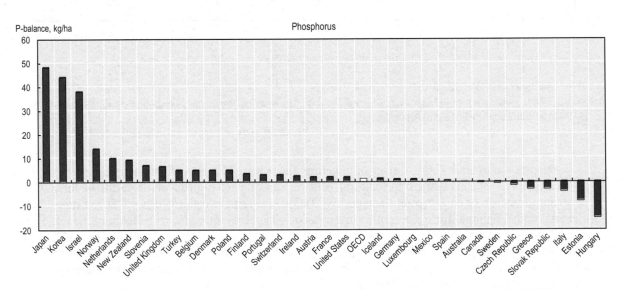

Source: OECD (2013), "Agri-Environmental Indicators: Environmental Performance of Agriculture 2013", *OECD Agriculture Statistics* (database).
DOI: 10.1787/data-00660-en.

StatLink ᴹˢᴾ http://dx.doi.org/10.1787/888933144711

Material productivity (biomass)

Policy context

Resource productivity and efficiency are high on the international policy agenda and are the focus of several national and international initiatives, such as the Kobe 3R Action Plan, the UNEP International Resource Panel and the EU 2020 Flagship initiative on resource efficiency. The OECD has two Council Recommendations related to advancing work in this area.

Monitoring progress

Monitoring natural resources – the way they are used in economic activity and contribute to economic outputs – and how their use impacts on the environment requires comprehensive data on natural resource flows and indicators that monitor progress.

Indicators based on Material Flows Analysis[4] are useful to measure progress with resource productivity. They also provide insights into the economic efficiency and environmental effectiveness with which materials are used in the production and consumption chain up to final disposal. A commonly used indicator is material productivity (or intensity), relating economic output to the amount of materials (or raw materials) used as inputs. It is defined as GDP per Domestic Material Consumption (DMC) or per Domestic Material Input (DMI).[5] It can be derived from Economy-Wide Material Flow Accounts[6] that cover the economy as a whole and distinguish between various material types and groups. Water as a resource is not covered in such accounts and needs to be reported separately.

Applying this approach to agriculture would require data on material flows broken down by industry, or alternatively data on major material inputs into agricultural activity and on material outputs from agricultural activity, including processed products. Such data are not yet available for all OECD countries and relevant indicators have yet to be defined.

Environmentally adjusted total factor productivity

Policy context

Central to examining green growth in agriculture is the inclusion of environmental externalities in growth accounting. Agricultural production affects natural resources and influences eco-systems and biodiversity. Many of these environmental effects exhibit the characteristics of negative or positive externalities or public goods, for which private markets do not exist or are poorly functioning. These effects are usually neglected in traditional growth accounting frameworks or in estimations of common indicators of economic performance, such as total factor productivity (TFP). By omitting these developments, traditional TFP – which is often interpreted as a measure of economic efficiency, competitiveness and a long-term determinant of material living standards – may be biased and lead to incorrect policy conclusions. Some of these problems can be addressed by developing a measure of total factor productivity that is adjusted for the use of natural resources and other environmental services.

Monitoring progress

As noted earlier, TFP is a well-defined measure of productivity but is usually computed as a residual and thus more difficult to communicate than partial productivity measures, such as labour productivity. Accounting for natural resource inputs and for emissions such as negative outputs would add an additional element of complexity. Nevertheless, this is considered to be a conceptually correct way of examining measurement bias that may arise from not recognising environmental services in traditional TFP measures.

Measurability

This indicator is not currently measurable and the OECD is researching ways to advance work in computing this indicator. The objective is to examine whether TFP growth has been under- or overstated as a consequence of omitting undesired outputs and natural resource inputs from the calculation (**Box 3.3**). The work will begin by focusing on integrating natural resources, such as land, timber, and sub-soil resources, into a set of inputs and on integrating undesirable outputs (selected emissions) into the set of outputs. OECD has also begun exploratory work on calculating environmentally-adjusted TFP for the agricultural and energy sectors.

Box 3.3. OECD's on-going work on adjusting total factor productivity estimates to account for environmental services

The OECD has developed a calculation method for adjusting TFP estimates to account for environmental services and applied it to selected countries. The work is based on the literature on productivity measurement with undesirable outputs (Pittman, 1983; Repetto et al. 1997). It integrates selected natural resources (land, timber, subsoil assets) as input factors and selected pollutant emissions (carbon dioxide, sulphur and nitrogen oxides) as undesirable "bad" outputs in the production function. The absence of data on resources, such as water and fish stocks, precludes their inclusion in the analysis at this stage.

The framework is based on a standard production function, whereby output is derived using labour and capital input factors. This function is complemented by natural capital and the negative effect of undesirable bad output on production. Two adjustments are made to the standard production function. First, natural capital inputs (including minerals, oil, gas, coal and timber) are aggregated into a natural resource index and enter the production function as a third input factor. Second, "bad outputs", essentially air pollutants, such as sulphur oxides and nitrogen oxides and CO_2 emissions are added to output to derive effective output.

The biggest challenge is data availability regarding the use of environmental inputs in production and the associated costs, in particular the cost of the depletion and degradation of natural resources and their use in consumption and production. As a first step, the techniques to compute the monetary value of natural resources are consistent with the 2008 SNA and the 2012 Central Framework of the SEEA. No attempt is made to estimate the value of other environmental services, particularly for "non-uses" such as regulating services. The SEEA Experimental Ecosystem Accounts will, in the longer term, provide further guidance on techniques for valuations.

Although subject to limitations in its practical implementation, this extension of productivity measurement can allow for a more accurate assessment of economic performance. Preliminary results of the OECD's work show that the adjustment of the traditional productivity growth measure for bad outputs is small. While this partly hinges on the fact that for lack of more comprehensive data only a limited set of bad outputs were considered – namely carbon dioxide, sulphur and nitrogen oxides – the relatively small adjustment of the traditional productivity growth measure is good news for two reasons. First, it implies that ignoring the bad outputs considered in this paper results in a relatively small bias of productivity measurement, and thus analysis based on traditional measures should be relatively reliable in this regard. Second, it also implies that the acceleration in productivity growth that would help to substantially reduce the bad outputs considered, without reducing output growth, should be possible to achieve.

Source: Brandt, N., P. Schreyer and V. Zipperer (2014), "Productivity Measurement with Natural Capital and Bad Output", *OECD Economics Department Working Papers*, No. 1154, OECD Publishing, Paris.

Notes

1. Agricultural GDP refers to gross agricultural production value in constant 2004-06 USD as reported in FAOSTAT.

2. Agricultural GDP refers to gross agricultural production value in constant 2004-06 USD as reported in FAOSTAT.

3. The *Life+ Agriclimatechange* project aims to develop a software tool to assess energy consumption and GHG emissions (*htwww.agriclimatechange.eu/index.php?lang=en*). This comprehensive tool is intended to be applicable throughout the whole of the European Union and was implemented between September 2010 and December 2013. Action plans were designed and implemented for farms located in the four participating countries (France, Germany, Italy and Spain).

4.   Material Flow Analysis (MFA) studies how natural resources and materials flows into, through and out of a given system (usually the economy) and how these flows interact with the economy and the environment. It is based on methodically organised physical flow accounts that provide data on the material inputs taken from the environment into the economy (e.g. resources extracted or harvested from the surrounding natural environment or imported from other countries), the transformation and use of inputs within the economy (from production to final consumption) and the material outputs from the economy to the environment as residuals (waste, pollutants) or to other countries in the form of exports. The data are compiled from available production, consumption and trade data, and from environment statistics (on waste, emissions, etc.).

5.   DMI measure the material inputs into an economy, accounting for the domestic extraction of materials and imports. DMC measures the amount of materials consumed in an economy (i.e. the direct apparent consumption of materials). It is composed of two elements, namely the domestic extraction and the physical trade balance (which equals imports minus exports). DMC equals DMI minus exports.

6.   MF accounts are part of the family of physical flow accounts described in the Central Framework of the System of Environmental Economic Accounts (SEEA). The SEEA has been adopted as an international statistical standard (UN, 2014). The reporting on economy-wide MF is mandatory in the European Union.

Bibliography

Brandt, N., P. Schreyer and V. Zipperer (2014), "Productivity Measurement with Natural Capital and Bad Outputs", *OECD Economics Department Working Papers*, No. 1154, OECD Publishing,
doi: http://dx.doi.org/0.1787/5jz0wh5t0ztd-en.

FAO, *FAOSTAT* (database), http://faostat.fao.org/.

International Fertiliser Association (IFA), *IFADATA* (database),
http://www.fertilizer.org/Statistics.

OECD (2014a), *Green Growth Indicators 2014*, OECD Green Growth Studies, OECD Publishing, Paris, doi: http://dx.doi.org/10.1787/9789264202030-en.

OECD (2014b), Decoupling trends: agricultural nutrient balances and agricultural production, in *Green Growth Indicators 2014*, OECD Publishing,
doi: http://dx.doi.org/10.1787/9789264202030-graph25-en.

OECD (2013a), *OECD Compendium of Agri-environmental Indicators,* OECD Publishing, Paris,
doi: http://dx.doi.org/10.1787/9789264186217-en.

OECD (2013b), "Agri-Environmental Indicators: Environmental Performance of Agriculture 2013", *OECD Agriculture Statistics* (database),
doi: http://dx.doi.org/10.1787/data-00660-en.

OECD (2010), *Sustainable Management of Water Resources in Agriculture*, OECD Publishing, Paris.
doi: http://dx.doi.org/10.1787/9789264083578-en.

OECD (2002), *Indicators to Measure Decoupling of Environmental Pressure from Economic Growth*, OECD general distribution document (SG/SD(2002)1/FINAL), Paris.

Pittman, R.W. (1983), "Multilateral Productivity Comparisons with Undesirable Outputs", *The Economic Journal*, Vol. 93, No. 372, pp. 883-891.

Repetto, R., D. Rothman, P. Faeth and D. Austin (1997), "Has Environmental Protection Really Reduced Productivity ", *Challenge*, Vol. 40(1), pp. 46-57.

Sorrell, S. (2009), "Jevons revisited: the events for backfire from improved energy efficiency", *Energy Policy*, Vol. 37, Issue 4.

Sorrell, S., J. Dimitropolous and M. Sommerville (2009), "Empirical estimates of direct rebound effects: A review", *Energy Policy*, Vol. 37, Issue 4.

United Nations (UN) (2014), *System of Environmental Economic Accounting – Central Framework*, European Commission, FAO, IMF, OECD, UN, the World Bank, United Nations, New York.

UNFCCC *Greenhouse Gas Inventory Data*, http://unfccc.int/ghg_data/items/3800.php.

United Nations Environment Programme (UNEP) (2011), *Decoupling and Sustainable Resource Management: Scoping the Challenges*, A Report of the Working Group on Decoupling to the International Resource Panel. M. Swilling and M. Fischer-Kowalski.

World Bank, *World Development Indicators (database)*, http://data.worldbank.org/data-catalog/world-development-indicators.

Chapter 4

Monitoring the impact of agriculture on the natural asset base and environmental quality of life

Chapter 4 focuses on the group of indicators relating to the natural asset base and the environmental quality of life. It examines the role that availability and the quality of freshwater, biological diversity and ecosystems, and the productivity of land and soil resources play in the development of green growth in agriculture. Due to data and methodological issues, no indicator that captures the impact of the environment on people's quality of life is proposed.

The statistical data for Israel are supplied by and under the responsibility of the relevant Israeli authorities. The use of such data by the OECD is without prejudice to the status of the Golan Heights, East Jerusalem and Israeli settlements in the West Bank under the terms of international law.

The group of indicators on *the natural asset base* aims to monitor whether the natural asset base is maintained – a condition for sustainable growth – because rising productivity may be associated with an increase in environmental pressures. Indicators in this group should be aligned with indicators of environmental and resource productivity, and focus on natural assets that matter the most to agricultural production. Consequently, indicators will vary across countries according to their natural asset base.

A major methodological question is the extent to which one type of asset can be substituted for another. Can, for example, an increase in land used for agricultural production offset the loss of a natural forest? As many natural assets are not (fully) priced, asset prices cannot adequately reflect society's preferences, which leads to under- or over-exploitation of these assets.

In principle, and for the purposes of indicator construction, social shadow prices (i.e. the social opportunity costs of the resources used) could be estimated, which could then be used to value the net investment of each natural asset. However, for natural assets, such as water and soil, the calculation of social shadow prices is not straightforward due to externalities and imperfect information about resource rents. In such cases, the physical evolution of natural assets could provide a starting point, although this alone would convey limited information about progress towards green growth. Indicators of stocks and flows of natural resources and environmental services need to be read along with information on resource management policies.

The main issues concerning green growth include the availability of freshwater and biological diversity and ecosystems, including species and habitat diversity, as well as the quality of land and soil resources. The following indicators are proposed.

Table 4.1. Indicators for monitoring the natural asset base

Theme	Indicators	Criteria			
		Capturing the nexus between the environment and the economy	Ease of communication for different users and audiences	Reflecting key global environmental issues	Measurable and comparable across countries
Renewable stocks	Freshwater resources				
	Share of agricultural freshwater withdrawal in total freshwater withdrawal	***	**	***	*
Biodiversity and ecosystem services	Land use resources				
	a) Land cover types, conversions and cover changes				
	Trends of arable land and cropland	***	***	***	***
	Trends of permanent pastures	***	***	***	***
	b) Soil resources				
	Share of agricultural land affected by water erosion classified as having moderate to severe water erosion risk	***	***	***	***
	Wildlife resources				
	Farm birds index	*	*	*	**

StatLink ⌷⌷ http://dx.doi.org/10.1787/888933144924

The group of indicators on *environmental quality of life* attempts to capture the direct impact of the environment on people's lives, in terms of: 1) exposure to various pollutants and the associated health effects; and 2) access to environmental services (e.g. water, sanitation, green space, etc.). Indicators in this group should be selected to reflect the most pressing environmental health risks associated with agricultural production. This should be mirrored in the presentation of information on environmental services or amenities. The OECD's economy-wide green growth indicators work includes two indicators: percentage of population exposed to air pollution and percentage of population using improved sanitation and waste water treatment facilities (OECD, 2014).

There are nevertheless serious issues related to data availability and methodology in constructing rigorous indicators in this area. The most obvious proxy indicators for agriculture relate to: 1) health risks to people associated with exposure to pesticides (e.g. number and rate of acute work-related poisonings due to pesticide exposure);[1] and 2) health risks to people associated with water pollution from agriculture. In both cases, data are incomplete (OECD, 2013). It could be argued that in OECD countries, environmental quality of life issues related to agricultural production are critical only in certain regions of countries. For these reasons, no indicator is proposed under this heading.

Renewable stocks: Freshwater

Policy context

Agriculture is the world's largest water user. Challenges involve sustainable management of water resources in agriculture (and other uses) by avoiding over-exploitation and degradation. Using more efficient technologies and applying the user-pays-principle and adopting an integrated approach to the management of freshwater resources are essential elements (OECD, 2010).

Monitoring progress

The indicators presented here relate to the trends in agriculture freshwater withdrawals and their share in total freshwater withdrawals.

When interpreting this indicator, it should be kept in mind that it only gives insights into quantitative aspects of water resources. Moreover, it is at the national level and may conceal significant territorial differences and should be complemented with information at the sub-national level. Finally, this indicator should be read in connection with indicators on cost-recovery ratios, water productivity and water quality.

Measurability

Indicators for agriculture water resources are limited. Information on freshwater resources can be derived from water resource accounts. This is available for several OECD countries, although the definitions and estimation methods employed may vary considerably from country to country and over time. More work is needed to improve the completeness and historical consistency of data on water abstractions, and the methods for estimating renewable water resources.

Main trends

Overall, withdrawals of freshwater resources by agriculture have declined in most OECD countries for which data are available (**Figure 4.1**). Moreover, agriculture's withdrawal of freshwater, expressed as a share in total withdrawals, has decreased in recent years as compared with the early-1990s, although it remains a major water user, accounting for over 40% of total withdrawals in nearly half of the OECD member countries (OECD, 2013).

Figure 4.1. Agricultural water withdrawals in selected OECD countries

Trends in agricultural freshwater withdrawals, 1995=100

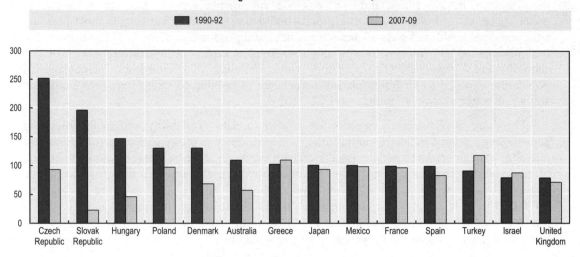

Share of agricultural freshwater withdrawals in total

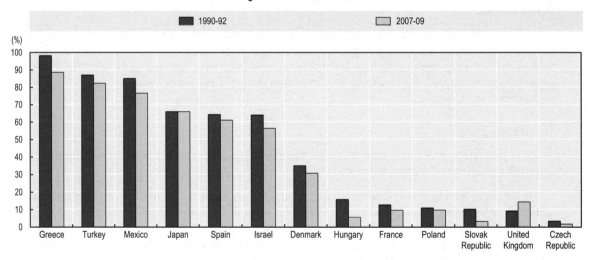

Note: 1994-95 for Belgium and Mexico.

Source: OECD (2013), "Agri-Environmental Indicators: Environmental Performance of Agriculture 2013", *OECD Agriculture Statistics* (database). doi: 10.1787/data-00660-en.

StatLink ⟲ http://dx.doi.org/10.1787/888933144726

The declining OECD trend in agricultural water withdrawals over the past decade was driven by a mix of factors, including: a near stable or reduction in the area irrigated (**Figure 3.12**); improvements in irrigation water management and technological efficiency; drought; release of water to meet environmental needs; and a slowdown in the growth of agricultural production (OECD, 2013).

Biodiversity and ecosystems

Policy context

Loss of biodiversity has been identified as one of the most pressing global environmental issues and its conservation is a key concern. Agriculture is crucial in biodiversity preservation as it is a major user of land and water resources that certain genetic resources and wild species depend on.

The way agricultural land is used and managed influences land cover and soil quality in terms of nutrient content and carbon storage. It affects water and air quality, determines erosion risks, plays a role in flood protection, and affects GHGs. The main challenge is to reconcile competing demands and conflicting interests sustainably and to preserve the land's essential ecosystem functions.

OECD countries employ a variety of policies and approaches designed to balance farm production and reduce harmful biodiversity impacts, especially those that affect wild species (e.g. birds) and ecosystems (e.g. wetlands). In addition, most OECD countries are signatories to international agreements of significance for agro-biodiversity conservation, such as the *Convention on Biological Diversity;* the *Convention on the Conservation of Migratory Species of Wild Animals*; and the *Ramsar Convention* for the protection of wetlands.

Monitoring progress

Development of a suitable indicator is beset with serious methodological and data difficulties. In the absence of such an indicator, the following proxy indicators – which relate to land use and cover, soil resources and wildlife resources – are proposed:

- *Land resources*: Changes in agricultural land use and land cover types – arable crops, permanent crops and pasture areas – are established environmental indicators. They represent a good proxy of the pressures on land-competing uses, as well as pressures on biodiversity. Although it does not directly measure biodiversity, it is considered as the best measure currently available to broadly monitor pressures on ecosystems and biodiversity.

- *Soil resources*: Agricultural land affected by water erosion classified as having moderate to severe water erosion risk.

- *Wildlife resources*: Farmland bird index.

Indicators on changes in agricultural land use and cover should be read in conjunction with changes on other types of land in the economy (e.g. forest, built-up areas, etc.), in order to obtain a more comprehensive picture of competing uses of land and potential pressures on ecosystems and biodiversity.

On wildlife resources, birds can act as "indicator species", providing a barometer of the health of the environment. Being close to (or at the top) of the food chain, they reflect changes in ecosystems rapidly compared to other species. The farmland bird index indicator measures populations of a selected group of breeding bird species that are dependent on agricultural land for nesting or breeding. In general, a decrease in the index means that the balance of bird species trend is negative, representing a biodiversity loss. Likewise, an increase in the index implies that the balance of bird species trend is positive, implying that biodiversity loss has halted. However, caution should be exercised in interpreting this indicator as an increasing farmland bird index may not always equate to an improving situation in the environment. In all cases, detailed analysis must be conducted to interpret accurately the indicator trends, while the composite index trend of farmland birds can hide important changes for individual species.

It should be noted that these indicators provide a partial picture only of the impact of agriculture on biodiversity. Furthermore, when making comparisons across countries, several factors should be taken into account including the level of economic development, the structure of agricultural production, countries' agricultural trade patterns, and geographical factors.

Measurability

Data on agricultural land use and cover exist for all OECD countries, although with varying degrees of quality. Internationally harmonised statistics on conversions from one type of land use to another are not yet available for non-agricultural land.

Data on threatened species are available for all OECD countries with varying degrees of completeness. The number of species known or assessed does not always accurately reflect the number of species in existence, and the definitions – which should follow International Union for Conservation of Nature (IUCN) standards – are applied with varying degrees of rigour in individual countries. Historical data are generally not comparable or are not available. Bird population indices are available for Europe and North America (Canada and the United States).

The indicator on agricultural land area classified as having moderate to severe water erosion, which is based on models, is subject to several limitations, making cross-country comparisons problematic. Moreover, comparable data are available for eight OECD countries only; in a number of countries where soil erosion or degradation is a widespread concern, there is little or no regular updating of national soil erosion monitoring (e.g. Australia, New Zealand, Portugal, Spain and Turkey) (OECD, 2013). For these reasons, results for this proposed indicator are not reported at this stage.

Main trends

In nearly all OECD countries the agricultural land area decreased over the 1990-2010 period in terms of both arable and crop land; permanent pasture area (which accounts for two-thirds of all OECD agricultural land) has declined in most countries (**Figure 4.2**). Agricultural land has mainly been converted to use for forestry and urban development (OECD, 2014; 2013). Despite this overall trend, agriculture remains the major land use for many countries, representing over 40% of the land area in two-thirds of OECD countries.

Permanent pasture, which represents a major share of agricultural semi-natural habitats, has declined most OECD countries. It has mainly been converted to forestry, although in some countries pasture has also been converted for cultivation of arable and permanent crops (e.g. Finland and the Netherlands).

The overall OECD trend masks some important differences between countries with a significant increase in permanent pasture area in countries which already had a high share of pasture in total agricultural land (e.g. Chile), and a sharp reduction in other countries where the permanent pasture share is also significant (e.g. Austria, the Netherlands and New Zealand).

Figure 4.2. Trends in agricultural land cover, change over the period 1990-2010 or most recent year

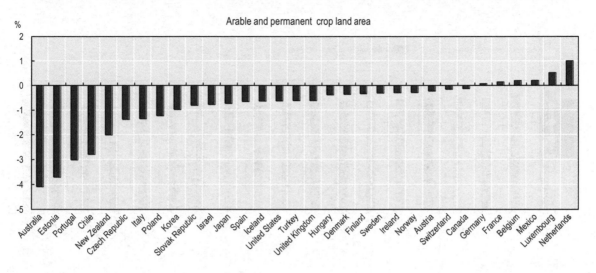

Note. Data for 2010 refer to the year 2009 for Austria, Canada and Israel; to the year 2008 for Chile and Italy.
Source: FAO, *FAOSTAT* (database), http://faostat.fao.org/.

StatLink 📊 http://dx.doi.org/10.1787/888933144733

Trends in OECD farmland bird populations declined continuously from 1990 to 2010 for almost all countries (**Figure 4.3**). But interpreting the consequences of changes in permanent pasture land areas for farmland birds and other wildlife species is complex. Without knowledge of the quality of the land change and its subsequent management, it is difficult to assess these developments. Given the magnitude of the decline in permanent pasture across most OECD countries over this period, however, it is likely that this has been one of the factors influencing the overall decline in farmland bird populations.

Figure 4.3. Farmland bird index in selected countries

2000=100

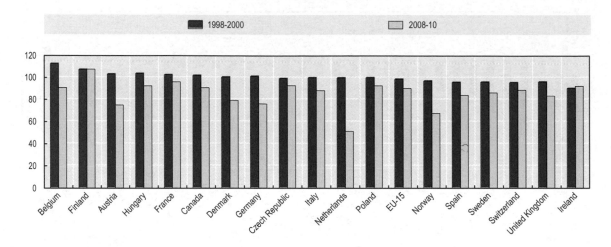

Source: OECD (2013), "Agri-Environmental Indicators: Environmental Performance of Agriculture 2013", *OECD Agriculture Statistics* (database). doi: 10.1787/data-00660-en.

StatLink ᯤ፰ᮤ *http://dx.doi.org/10.1787/888933144744*

The assessment of land use changes both between agriculture (e.g. pasture and arable crops) and other uses of land (e.g. forestry, urban use), and between pasture and arable crops is incomplete due to the paucity of datasets. A complete analysis of changes, including data on how different land types are managed and influence the wild flora and fauna that inhabit farmland, was not possible.

Note

1.   See, for example, Minnesota Department of Health, *Acute Work-Related Pesticide Associated Illness and Injury Reported to Poison Control Centers*, www.health.state.mn.us/divs/hpcd/cdee/occhealth/indicators/pesticide.html.

Bibliography

OECD (2014), *Green Growth Indicators 2014*, OECD Green Growth Studies, OECD Publishing, Paris,
doi: http://dx.doi.org/10.1787/9789264202030-en.

OECD (2013), "Agri-Environmental Indicators: Environmental Performance of Agriculture 2013", *OECD Agriculture Statistics* (database),
doi: .http://dx.doi.org/10.1787/data-00660-en.

OECD (2010), *Sustainable Management of Water Resources in Agriculture*, OECD Studies on Water, OECD Publishing, Paris,
doi: http://dx.doi.org/10.1787/9789264083578-en.

Chapter 5

Monitoring policy responses and economic opportunities in agriculture

The category of indicators included in this chapter aims to identify the effectiveness of policy in delivering green growth and the economic opportunities arising from such growth. They should also help to identify potential synergies and trade-offs among different policy objectives, and among green growth goals.

The statistical data for Israel are supplied by and under the responsibility of the relevant Israeli authorities. The use of such data by the OECD is without prejudice to the status of the Golan Heights, East Jerusalem and Israeli settlements in the West Bank under the terms of international law.

There is a broad category of indicators that aims to discern both the effectiveness of policy in delivering green growth and the economic opportunities which arise from such growth. These indicators should help identify potential synergies and trade-offs among different policy objectives, and among green growth goals. It combines two types of indicators: i) policies of importance to green growth; and ii) economic opportunities arising from green growth. In the OECD framework on monitoring progress towards green growth, these issues are treated together, as they can be relevant for all elements included in the green growth framework: the natural asset base, productivity and environmental quality of life.

Identifying indicators in this group is difficult. A wide range of opportunities and policy responses is possible, including those related to government transfers, prices and taxes, regulations, technology and innovation, management approaches, and training and skills development. These thematic areas are of varying relevance across countries.

On policy responses, indicators should capture the policy measures contained in the *Green Growth Policy Toolkit* for food and agriculture (see OECD, 2013a; **Table 5.1**). The OECD Producer and Consumer Support Estimates (PSE/CSE) database contains rich data and indicators on various agricultural support policies which are of direct relevance to green growth. This database can be used, for example, to construct indicators of the extent to which agricultural support policies are becoming less harmful/more beneficial to the environment, as well as to calculate indicators on market distortions associated with agricultural policies and the share of public investments in R&D.

Indicators on government transfers to producers should be complemented with indicators reflecting regulatory measures put in place by governments to reduce the negative effects of agriculture on the environment. The construction of such indicators is, however, constrained by important conceptual issues and data gaps (i.e. information is often of a qualitative nature).

Identifying indicators on the aspect of economic opportunities arising from green growth is perhaps the most challenging, not only from the point of view of data availability, but also on conceptual grounds. The main opportunities which could arise relate to: i) technology development and innovation, which, as was noted earlier, are key determinants of agricultural growth and productivity, and are crucial for moving towards a resource-efficient, low-carbon agricultural sector; and ii) green entrepreneurship, training and the development of skills. All of these are important factors to help farmers adopt innovations that **minimise the environmentally detrimental effects of agricultural production (among the foremost of these are integrated pest management, integrated plant nutrient systems, and no-till/conservation agriculture).**

Developing indicators to monitor technology and innovation relevant to green growth in agriculture is complex due to the difficulty in providing an unequivocal definition for "green" innovation or technology both at the sectoral and economy-wide levels. There is no systematic measure of the impact of innovation on the economy or of the impact of policies on innovation. As innovations become more diverse and complex, it becomes increasingly difficult to measure the various facets of innovation.

In addition, conventional indicators capture only part of the innovation process. For example, input indicators measure investment in innovation, such as R&D expenditures and the number of staff. Output measures include the number of publications and quotations in academic journals, or the number of patents registered. However, patents are an indicator of invention rather than innovation, since not all patents are commercialised and it is not possible to patent some types of innovation in the agricultural sector. The limits of bibliographic indicators are obvious.

Table 5.1. Green growth toolkit for food and agriculture

	Green growth policies
Environmental regulations and standards	Enact and enforce controls on excessive use of agrochemicals and fertilisers in production
	Strengthen rules and standards for water, soil quality, and land management
	Improve enforcement of environmental regulations and standards and certification from the farm-gate to the retail sector
Support measures	Decouple farm support from commodity production levels and prices
	Remunerate provision of environmental public goods (such as biodiversity, carbon sequestration, and flood and drought control) beyond reference level and closely targeted to environmental outcomes[1]
	Target environmental outcomes where feasible, otherwise target production practices favourable to the environment
	Target public investments in green technologies
Economic instruments	Price inputs to reflect scarcity value of natural resources
	Impose charges/taxes on use of environmentally-damaging inputs
	Implement trading schemes for water rights and carbon emissions
	Address policy constraints (governance, etc.) in less developed economies
Trade measures	Lower tariff and non-tariff barriers on food and agriculture products bearing in mind the potential impact on environmental concerns such as biodiversity and sustainable resource use.
	Eliminate export subsidies and restrictions on agricultural products
	Support, well-functioning input and output markets
Research and development	Increase public research on sustainable food and agricultural systems
	Promote private agricultural R&D through grants and tax credits
	Undertake public/private partnerships for green agricultural research
Development assistance	Allocate more development aid for environmentally sustainable initiatives, in food and agriculture
	Raise profile of agriculture in Poverty Reduction Strategies
	Allocate more funding for agriculture in Aid for Trade projects
Information, education, training and advice	Increase public awareness for more sustainable patterns of consumption such as via eco-labelling and certification
	Incorporate sustainable approaches in training, education and advice programmes throughout the entire food chain

Source: OECD (2013), *Policy Instruments to Support Green Growth in Agriculture*, OECD Green Growth Studies, OECD Publishing, Paris. doi: 10.1787/9789264203525-en.

Moreover, data on the level of technology and innovation in agriculture, as measured by conventional indicators (such as expenditure on green technologies) and the number of patents are not available for most countries. In general, aspects related to green innovation and investments in agriculture are inadequately captured by the currently available indicators and merit further development.

In the same vein, indicators for the creation of "green jobs" are subject to conceptual difficulties and are not part of the OECD green growth headline indicators. For example, an indicator on employment creation generated by green technologies (e.g. renewable energy technologies) should take into account all employment effects (direct and indirect).[2] Overall, monitoring of this area is considered to be the weakest in terms of data availability and relevant quantifiable indicators.

With the aforementioned considerations in mind, indicators are proposed for the following issues of importance to green growth (**Table 5.2**).

- *Transfers, taxes and prices* that provide important signals to producers and consumers are tools to internalise externalities and to influence the behaviour of market participants towards more environmentally-friendly patterns.

- *Investment in human capital* which facilitates the uptake and dissemination of technology and knowledge and contributes to meeting economic growth and environmental objectives.

- *Technology and innovation* important drivers of growth and productivity in general, and of green growth in particular.

Monitoring policy responses

Policy context

A central challenge to achieving green growth is to ensure that all costs associated with economic activities are reflected in production and consumption decisions (i.e. that they are internalised either through prices or via some other mechanism). Governments have at their disposal a wide range of potential policies that influence the productive efficiency and environmental performance of agriculture.

Government policies, for example, have long provided transfers (or support) either directly or indirectly to the agricultural sector in OECD economies. This is in addition to a wide array of regulations, some of which are economy-wide, others more specific to the sector. The role of market-based instruments, such as taxes and charges and tradable permit systems in promoting green growth in agriculture is not, however, as prominent as in other sectors (e.g. transport).

The policy challenge is to find cost-effective ways to account for environmental externalities that are not factored into producer and consumer decisions. This implies addressing at least three policy sets: removing those transfers that distort production decisions and trade flows, and harm the environment (or cause extra pressure on natural resources); enforcing the polluter-pays-principle; and finding ways to incentivise producers to generate economic and environmental services (benefits). The types of transfer measures that are most likely to create the greatest barriers to improving economic efficiency (and thus potentially to growth) and increasing environmental performance should be prime targets for policy reform.

Monitoring progress

The following indicators are proposed:

- Trends of the potentially most environmentally harmful support to farmers.

- Trends of the level and relative importance of environmentally-related taxes on agriculture (%).

- Water pricing and cost recovery.

Table 5.2. Indicators for monitoring green growth policies and opportunities

Theme	Indicators	Criteria			
		Capturing the nexus between the environment and the economy	Ease of communication to different users and audiences	Reflecting key global environmental issues	Measurable and comparable across countries
Policy responses	Government transfers to producers				
	Trends of potentially the most environmentally harmful producer support	***	***	***	***
	Environmentally related taxes in agriculture				
	Share of agriculture in energy taxes	***	***	***	**
	Share of agriculture in transport taxes	***	***	***	**
	Share of agriculture in pollution taxes	***	***	***	**
	Effective tax rates on energy for agriculture	***	***	***	**
	Water pricing and recovery	***	***	***	**
	Supplementary indicators				
	Trends of total support to farmers	**	***	**	***
	Trends of the potentially most environmentally beneficial producer support	***	***	**	***
Economic opportunities	Empowering people to innovate				
	Farmers with agricultural training	***	***	n.a.	**
	Trends of payments on agricultural training and education	***	***	n.a.	***
	Supplementary indicators				
	Age structure of farmers (share of young and elderly farmers in total)	**	***	n.a.	***
	Enrolment rates of farmers in tertiary education	**	***	n.a.	**
	Conservation technical assistance	**	***	**	**
	Investing in green innovation				
	Trends of agricultural R&D payments in total support to agriculture	**	***	n.a.	*
	Share of agricultural green innovation (patents) in total green innovation (patents of importance to GG)	***	***	***	**
	Supplementary indicators				
	Share of payments on agricultural R&D in total support to agriculture	***	***	*	***
	Share of R&D (private and public) on agriculture in total R&D expenditures	***	***	*	**

*** = High; ** = Medium; * = Low; n.a. = Not applicable.

The share of the potentially most environmentally harmful support in total support, the composition of environmentally-related taxes in agriculture (energy, transport, pollution and resources) and effective tax rates on energy use are proposed as supplementary indicators. In addition, the indicator on the potentially most environmentally harmful support should be read in connection with indicators of the level of total producer support, while the indicator on agriculture's contribution to environmentally-related tax revenues can be read in conjunction with indicators on GHG emissions. The potentially most harmful support to farmers comprises the following (OECD, 2013a):

- Market price support.

- Payments based on commodity output, without imposing environmental constraints on farming practices.

- Payments based on variable input use, without imposing environmental constraints on farming practices

Since the mid-1980s, as part of its work on monitoring and evaluating agricultural policy developments, the OECD has measured on an annual basis the level and composition of support (monetary transfers) associated with agricultural policies in OECD countries (and, to an increasing extent, also for non-OECD countries), using a standard methodology. The classification of support into different categories is based on how policies are actually implemented and not on the objectives or impacts of those policies.

It should be emphasised that neither the total PSE nor its composition in terms of different categories of policies can be interpreted as indicating the actual impact of a policy on production and markets (OECD, 2013a). Clearly, the actual impacts (*ex post*) will depend on the many factors that determine the aggregate degree of responsiveness of farmers to policy changes, including any constraints on production. For example, while it is true that market price support mechanisms and payments based on output are potentially the most harmful for the environment, whether they actually are harmful depends on a host of other factors, including whether production quotas are attached to them and whether they incorporate strong cross-compliance requirements or are constrained by agri-environmental regulations independent of the support payments. Similarly, payments based on area, animal numbers, farm receipts or income, and historical entitlements are only potentially neutral in their effects on the environment, but may be harmful − or even beneficial − depending on specific programme designs and other regulations (OECD, 2013a).

Information on environmentally-related taxes is available from the OECD-EEA database on instruments used for environmental policy and natural resources management (www2.oecd.org/ecoinst/queries/). Information on energy taxes is available from the IEA. EUROSTAT also publishes environmental taxes by economic activity, following the SEEA Framework for European countries at NAC Rev 2 level (data include forestry). Data on effective taxes only account for taxes imposed at the federal level.

Measurability

Data for the indicators on government transfers to producers are published annually by OECD (PSE/CSE database) for OECD countries and for certain non-OECD partner economies. For the European Union, the data refer to the European Union as a whole and no data are available for individual EU member countries.

The *System of Environmental-Economic Accounting: Central Framework* provides a definition of environmentally-related taxes (UN, 2014). In the SEEA, the tax base is used to define whether a tax is environmental. Specifically, an environmental tax is a tax whose tax base is a physical unit (or a proxy of it) of something that has a proven, specific, negative impact on the environment.[3] The SEEA Framework groups environmental taxes into four categories:

- *Energy taxes*: Taxes on energy products used for both transport and stationary purposes (i.e. fuel oils, natural gas, coal and electricity).

- *Transport taxes*: Taxes related to the ownership and use of motor vehicles.

- *Pollution taxes:* Taxes on measured or estimated emissions to air and water, and the generation of solid waste. An exception is taxes on carbon, which are included under energy taxes. Taxes on sulphur are included in this category.

- *Resource taxes*: Typically includes taxes on water abstraction, extraction of raw materials and other resources (e.g. sand and gravel).

Effective tax rates on energy are taken from a recent OECD study (OECD, 2013c). This study provides the first time a systematic comparative analysis of the structure and level of taxes on energy use in all OECD countries. It also presents effective tax rates on energy use in terms of both energy content and carbon emissions for the full range of energy sources and uses in each country. Fuel quantities are expressed in terms of energy value (in gigajoules – GJ), reflecting that what all the products have in common is that they are sources of energy. The quantities of the various energy sources are expressed in terms of the carbon emissions associated with their use (in tonnes of CO_2).

Concerning water pricing, there is an important data gap which prevents comparison of trends across countries and over time. Comprehensive data on water pricing and cost recovery are not available. Overall, this aspect of monitoring green growth is considered to be the weakest in terms of data availability and relevant quantifiable indicators.

Main trends

Government transfers to producers

OECD countries have made a concerted effort to reduce the most environmentally harmful types of agricultural supports and have achieved a decrease from over 85% of the total in 1990-92 to 49% in 2010-12 (**Figure 5.1**). The largest decrease of the share of the potentially environmentally most harmful support was observed in Australia and in the European Union (**Figure 5.2**). This share increased only in New Zealand, which is explained by the fact that it has consistently the lowest level of support (i.e. the percentage Producer Support Estimate is 1%) and its agriculture is driven by market signals.[4]

While some countries have taken clear steps to decouple support from output and price levels, other countries have not yet begun to address the problem. The potentially most environmentally beneficial support increased its share in total support to producers, but on average accounts for only 8% in the OECD area.[5]

Figure 5.1. Evolution of producer support by potential environmental impact in the OECD area

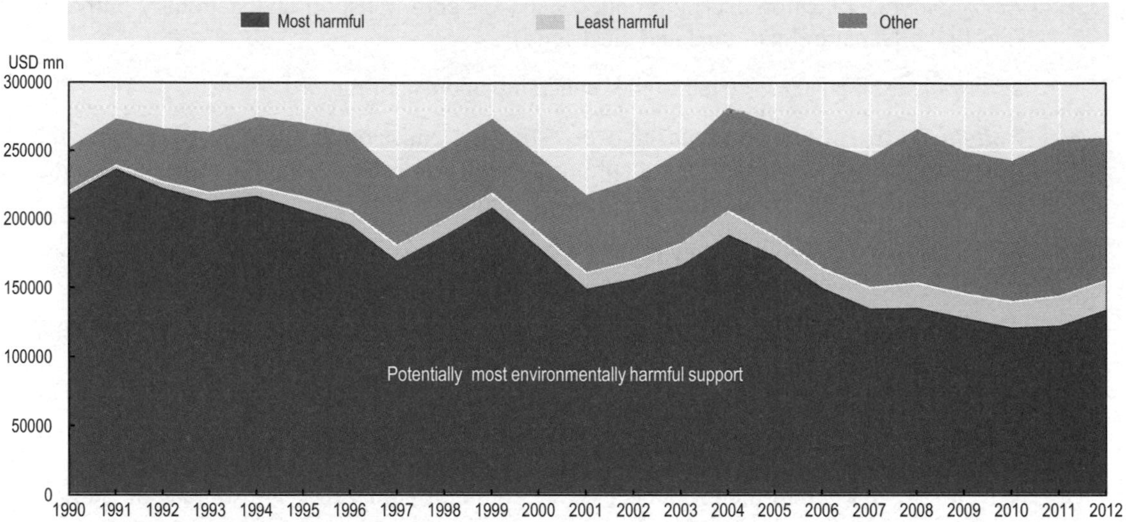

Source: OECD (2013), *"Producer and Consumer Support Estimates", OECD Agriculture Statistics Database*, http://dx.doi.org/10.1787/agr-pcse-data-en.

StatLink ᵃᵍ http://dx.doi.org/10.1787/888933144751

Environmental taxes

Environmental taxes (or charges) are policy measures imposing a tax relating to pollution or environmental degradation, including taxes on farm inputs (or outputs) that are a potential source of environmental damage. Environment-related taxes, by influencing the behaviour of producers and consumers, constitute an important instrument for governments to internalise the environmental externalities of economic activity ("pricing externalities") and raise revenues. Specific taxes on energy, for example, alter the relative prices of different forms of energy and thus alter patterns of energy use, with important economic and environmental consequences. They also affect net income and have important distributional implications.

Only a few countries have levied taxes and charges on farm inputs as a way to address environmental issues in agriculture. These have mostly been applied to environmentally-damaging chemicals, such as those associated with commercial fertiliser and pesticide use. This may at least partly reflect the practical problems of measurement; unlike other sectors where pollution can normally be monitored at "point", the pollution from agriculture is much more widely dispersed, as it tends to originate from many different farms and in varying intensities.

Although environment-related taxes in agriculture (including forestry) have increased in all countries for which data are available, their contribution to total environment-related tax revenues was lower than 5% in all countries reported (**Figure 5.3**). Looking at the contribution of the individual components, total energy and transport tax revenues were lower than 6% in all countries reported; while for pollution they were between 7% and 10% in two countries, and less than 1% in the remaining seven countries (**Figure 5.4**). It is noteworthy that while the agricultural sector in the OECD area on average pays around 6% of energy taxes, it accounts for 8% of net GHG emissions in the total economy.

Figure 5.2. Producer support by potential environmental impact in OECD countries

Share in total producer support (%)

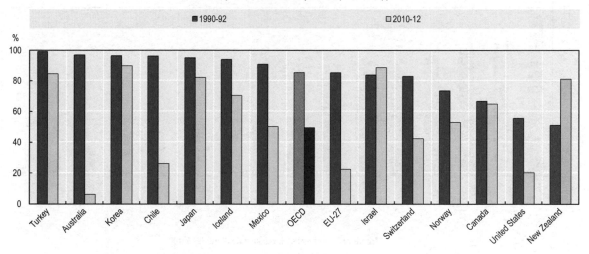

Potentially most environmentally harmful producer support

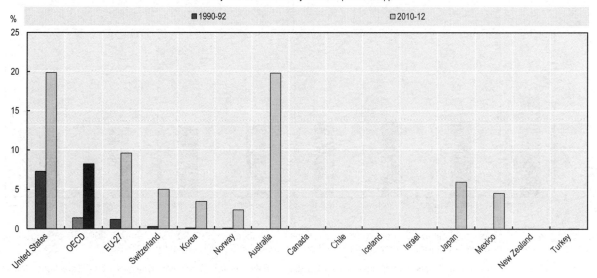

Potentially most environmentally beneficial producer support

Note: 1995-97 for Israel, instead of 1990-92.

Source: OECD (2013), "Producer and Consumer Support Estimates", *OECD Agriculture Statistics Database*, http://dx.doi.org/10.1787/agr-pcse-data-en.

StatLink ᴍ� http://dx.doi.org/10.1787/888933144762

Figure 5.3. Environmental taxes in agriculture

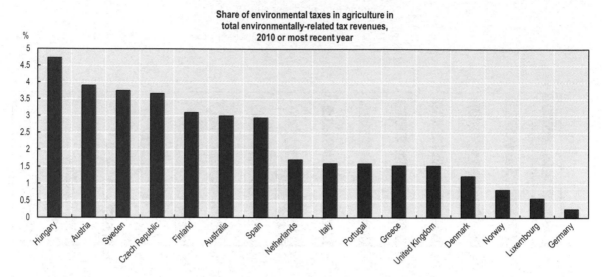

Share of environmental taxes in agriculture in
total environmentally-related tax revenues,
2010 or most recent year

Trends of environmental taxes in agriculture, 1995=100

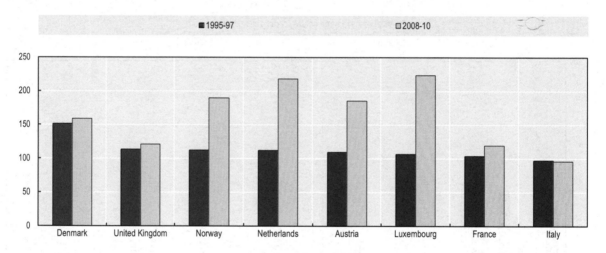

Notes: In the upper panel, for United Kingdom 1995-97 average is replaced by 1997-99; for Denmark 2008-10 average refer to 2008 data. In the lower panel, data for Denmark and Finland are for 2008. Data include forestry; NAC REV2.

Source: EUROSTAT; Australian Bureau of Statistics (ABS) (2013), *Towards the Australian Environmental-Economic Accounts*, Information Paper, Canberra.

StatLink ᴍᴤ￼ http://dx.doi.org/10.1787/888933144777

Figure 5.4. Environmental taxes in agriculture by type: Share in total (%), 2010 or most recent year

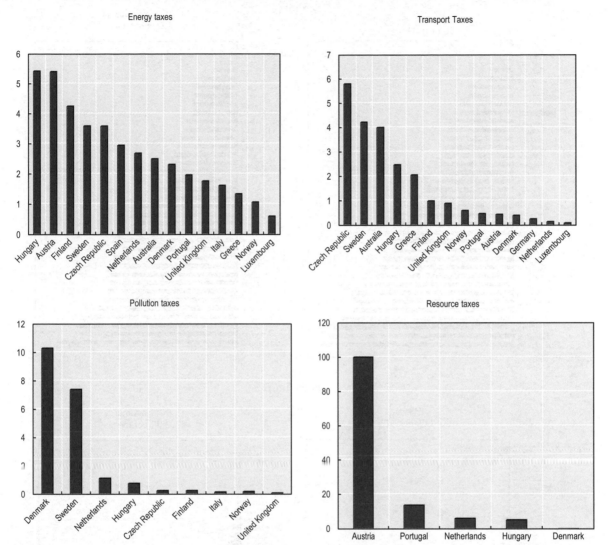

Note: Data for Denmark and Finland are for 2008. Data include forestry; NAC REV2.

Source: EUROSTAT; Australian Bureau of Statistics (ABS) (2013), *Towards the Australian Environmental-Economic Accounts*, Information Paper, Canberra.

StatLink ⟲ http://dx.doi.org/10.1787/888933144784

Taxes on energy use are by far the single most important source of environmental tax revenue from agriculture. In 2010, energy taxes on agriculture accounted for more than 90% of environmental tax revenue from agriculture (e.g. Austria, Czech Republic, Italy and Spain). **Figure 5.5** sets out for each country (for the economy as a whole and for agriculture) the overall average effective tax rate, on a weighted basis on energy use (left panel) and on CO_2 emissions from energy use (right panel). Both at an economy-wide and agricultural sectoral level, there are significant differences in the overall level of energy taxation across the OECD area.

Figure 5.5. Tax rates on energy and CO₂ from energy

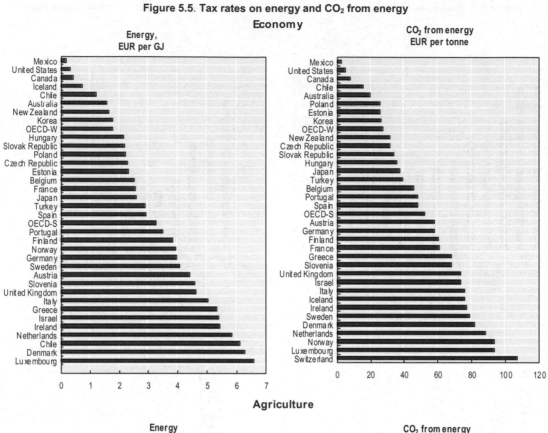

Note: Energy: Left panels; CO₂: Right panels.

Tax rates are as of 1 April 2013. Further details on the methodology can be found in the source. OECD-S = OECD area simple average; OECD-W= OECD area weighted average.

Source: OECD (2013), *Taxing Energy Use: A Graphical Analysis*, OECD Publishing. doi: 10.1787/9789264183933-en.

StatLink ⧉ http://dx.doi.org/10.1787/888933144797

Overall, tax rates on energy use for the whole economy are much higher than those imposed on agriculture. One of the reasons for this is that fuel used in agriculture is often exempt from tax. Fuel tax exemptions provide no signal with respect to external costs, thereby encouraging over-use. In energy terms, the simple average rate on agriculture is almost half the rate on the whole economy (EUR 3.28 per GJ for the whole economy and (EUR 1.81 per GJ), while the differences are smaller in terms of weighted average rate (1.77 per GJ for the whole economy and 1.22 per GJ for agriculture). The range of country averages, however, is very wide: from EUR 8.91 per GJ in Ireland to zero in Australia, Chile, Mexico and the United States.

Similarly, there is a wide range of effective tax rates on carbon (as set out in the right panel of **Figure 5.5**). The simple average rate on agriculture is EUR 26.83 per tonne of CO_2, while the weighted average is EUR 20.85 per tonne of CO_2. These rates are much lower than the corresponding rates for the whole economy. Again, there is a wide range around these averages: from zero in Chile and the United States to EUR 124.79 per tonne in Ireland. Overall, the highest rates for agriculture are observed in Ireland, Denmark, the Netherlands, the Slovak Republic and Norway.

Water pricing and cost recovery

Given the anticipated growth in demand for food and water and increasing pressures from climate change, agriculture will be a key target for policy makers, as it consumes about 70% of the world's total freshwater withdrawals (45% in OECD countries). OECD work shows that the level of charges for water supplied to farms has risen in OECD countries (OECD, 2010).

Frequently, farmers only pay the operational and maintenance costs for water supplied, and there is little or no recovery of agriculture's share of the capital costs of water infrastructure (**Table 5.3**). Where countries have raised water charges to farmers, available evidence indicates this has not led to reduced agricultural output. However, water charges rarely reflect scarcity and social values or environmental costs and benefits.

Table 5.3. Full supply cost recovery for surface water delivered on-farm, 2008

Supply cost recovery	Country
Full cost recovery of operation and maintenance, and capital costs	Austria, Denmark, Finland, New Zealand, Sweden, United Kingdom
Full cost recovery of operation and maintenance, but partial recovery of capital costs	Australia, Canada, France, Japan, United States
Partial cost recovery of operation and maintenance, and recovery of capital costs	Greece, Hungary, Ireland, Italy, Mexico, Netherlands, Poland, Portugal, Spain, Switzerland, Turkey
Partial cost recovery of operation and maintenance, with capital costs fully supported	Korea

Notes:

Full supply costs recovery for water deliveries to farms include: operation and maintenance costs (e.g. maintaining and repairing the irrigation infrastructure) and capital costs, both renewal capital costs (e.g. replacing irrigation canals) and new capital costs (e.g. constructing dams).

No information is available for the following OECD countries: Belgium; the Czech Republic; Germany; Iceland, Luxembourg, Norway, the Slovak Republic.

StatLink ᴍᴏᴩ http://dx.doi.org/10.1787/888933144949

Monitoring economic opportunities

Policy context

The capacity of the agricultural sector to produce adequate supplies of food and feed in an environmentally sound manner is closely linked to the level of technological development and innovation. The strong growth in agricultural productivity experienced since the post-war period has been driven largely by technological advances and the rapid adoption and diffusion of new technologies.

Green growth can provide a new paradigm for agricultural research and innovation, placing the emphasis simultaneously on environmental and economic requirements with the aim of enhancing productivity without compromising the natural resource capital. Technologies that can contribute to an economically efficient farm sector and provide financial viability for farmers, while at the same time improving environmental performance in a way that is acceptable to society, will provide "triple dividends" to green growth. The main challenges are to strengthen research, foster innovation and the use of new technologies in production, and encourage the creation of markets and the uptake of new technologies by consumers.

Monitoring progress

Monitoring progress towards green growth in agriculture can be assessed through proxy indicators on empowering people to innovate and on investing in green innovation. As shown in **Table 5.2**, in the sub-category empowering people to innovate, the proxy indicators proposed are: trends in expenditure on agricultural training and education; and the share of farm managers with basic or full education in agriculture attained. In addition, the age structure of farmers (share of young and elderly farmers in total); the enrolment rates of farmers in tertiary education; and trends in conservation technical assistance are proposed as supplementary indicators.

For the investing in green innovation sub-category, progress towards green growth can be assessed through proxy indicators of innovation. R&D expenditure (public and private) and patent applications of importance to green growth are the two most common indicators used (OECD, 2014).

Unfortunately, data on environmentally-related R&D expenditure across countries are not available for agriculture, while data on patents important to green growth are limited. Consequently, the following proxy indicators are proposed:

- Share of farmers with agricultural training.

- Trends of payments on agricultural training and education.

- Trends in government R&D expenditure on agriculture.

- Trends in patents in environmentally-related technologies. This entails patent applications in agriculture under Patent Co-operation Treaty (PCT) of waste management, renewable energy generation and of water management.

    Supplementary proxy indicators might include:

    o   Government budget appropriations or outlays for R&D (GBAORD) on agriculture (share in total).

    o   Business sector expenditure for R&D on agriculture (share in total).

    o   Share of government R&D expenditure on agriculture in total support to agriculture.[6]

While interpretation of the proposed indicator on empowering people to innovate is straightforward, analysis of the trends of the indicators on investing in green innovation should be exercised with caution. First, R&D expenditure is an input measure that indicates an economy's relative degree of investment in generating new knowledge and it does not reflect a green growth outcome. Second, cross-country comparisons should consider differences among countries in industrial structure and research capabilities; high R&D spending alone does not warrant a superior innovation performance (OECD, 1995).

Third, patent applications reflect inventive performance, but not all technologies or processes are the subject of patent applications, and not all enterprises wish to disclose their technological advances through patent applications. Also, patents may or may not lead to innovation. The development and adoption of new technologies with positive green growth implications may come from across all sectors of the economy. The patent indicators here do not measure the full extent of innovative activities and do not distinguish between high-quality and low-quality patents.

Finally, it should be noted that investigation of the influence of agricultural policies (and their reform) on productivity growth, and the generation and diffusion of technology in the agricultural sector should be performed with caution since the relationship is complex and the existence of a correlation between productivity rates and policies does not imply causality (OECD, 1995).

Measurability

Data on agricultural training and education are published by EUROSTAT (Farm Structure Surveys) and by agricultural censuses of countries. The proposed indicator – share of farm managers with basic or full education in agriculture attained – provides information on the education level of farm managers within a region. This indicator covers managers of non-group holdings who have attained basic or full agricultural training.

The farm manager's agricultural training is defined by EUROSTAT as follows:

- *Only practical agricultural experience*: Experience acquired through practical work on an agricultural holding.

- *Basic agricultural training*: Any training courses completed at a general agricultural college and/or an institution specialising in certain subjects (including horticulture, viticulture, sylviculture, pisciculture, veterinary science, agricultural technology and associated subjects). A completed agricultural apprenticeship is regarded as basic training.

- *Full agricultural training*: Any training course continuing for the equivalent of at least two years' full-time training after the end of compulsory education and completed at an agricultural college, university or other institute of higher education in agriculture, horticulture, viticulture, sylviculture, pisciculture, veterinary science, agricultural technology or an associated subject.

Data on government payments that finance agricultural training and education are published in the OECD PSE/CSE database. These data, which are part of the General Service Support Estimate expenditures, can underestimate government efforts to support education and training to farmers as they only include transfers to producers collectively (i.e. services that benefit agriculture but whose incidence is not at the level of individual farmers). On-farm advisory services and technical assistance are not included.[7]

The OECD PSE/CSE database also publishes annual data on government R&D and extension expenditures on agriculture for OECD countries. The OECD database on *Science, Technology and Patent* contains data on R&D and patent applications. R&D expenditures include gross domestic expenditure on R&D by sector of performance (e.g. higher education, government, business and private non-profit), by field of science and socio-economic objective (e.g. environment, energy, etc.), as well government budget appropriations and outlays for R&D (GBAORD). Data on GBAORD are available for most OECD countries, but significant gaps exist concerning harmonised data on private-sector R&D expenditures, as well as harmonised micro-data.

Government budget appropriations or outlays for R&D (GBAORD) measure the funds committed by the federal/central government for R&D. This can be broken down by various socioeconomic objectives, including control and care for the environment. For more information, see the OECD Project on Environmental Policy and Corporate Behaviour (*www.oecd.org/env/cpe/firms*).

Determining whether an innovation is environmental or not is a question of degree and not of kind. The OECD publishes data on patent applications under the Patent Co-operation Treaty (PCT) which are of importance to green growth. More specifically, a search algorithm developed by the OECD Secretariat and the European Patent Office (EPO) was used to generate data on environmental technology patent applications. The data cover technologies for pollution abatement (air pollution control, water pollution control and wastewater treatment) and for waste management, recycling and prevention. For further details on classifications, see *www.oecd.org/environment/innovation/indicator*.

The link between patents and the scientific literature is based on an analysis of the "non-patent literature" (NPL) listed in patent documents. NPL includes peer-reviewed scientific papers, conference proceedings, databases and other literature.[8] The selection is based on the international patent classification code. For more information on patents data and methodology see OECD (2009) *Patent Statistics Manual*, www.oecd.org/science/inno/oecdpatentstatisticsmanual.htm

From these aggregate categories, the following items were identified for agriculture: fertilisers from waste; and energy generation from fuels of non-fossil origin (biofuels and fuel from waste, for example, methane) under the renewable energy generation. For technologies with climate change mitigation potential, the data are too aggregated and technologies relevant to agriculture cannot be identified.

Concerning data on green innovations related to water, new OECD work provides the first descriptive analysis of innovation in water-related adaptation technologies and of their international diffusion at the global level (Dechezleprêtre, Haščič and Johnstone, 2013). The analysis is based on a unique data set comprised of over 50 000 patents filed in 83 patent offices, between 1990 and 2010, and covers a wide range of technologies that may either increase the supply of water in drought conditions (e.g. rainwater collection, groundwater collection, water storage, desalination, etc., or decrease water consumption (e.g. water control in agriculture, drought-resistant crops, drip irrigation, water efficiency technologies in power production, domestic water recycling, efficient water distribution systems, etc.). These three water-related technologies are defined as follows:

- *Drought-resistant crops*: Mutation or genetic engineering; DNA or RNA concerning genetic engineering, vectors (e.g. plasmids, or their isolation, preparation or purification for drought, cold, or salt resistance).

- *Drip irrigation*: Watering arrangements located above the soil which make use of perforated pipe-lines or pipe-lines with dispensing fittings.

- *Controlled watering*: Watering arrangements making use of perforated pipe-lines located beneath soil level.

Main trends

Training and education

Better educated and trained farm managers are more likely to make successful changes to farm-management practices and be more innovative (Labarth and Laurent, 2009). The results presented here include European OECD member countries only (i.e. OECD member countries that are also members of the European Union, Iceland, Norway and Switzerland). Learning by doing is the main form of training for the majority of the farmers as the majority of the farm managers have acquired agricultural experience through practical work (**Table 5.4**).

Table 5.4. Training and education in agriculture in selected OECD countries (% of farm managers)

	Farm managers with agricultural training				Farm managers with practical experience only	
	Basic training		Full training			
	2005	2010	2005	2010	2005	2010
Austria	19.7	22.4	28.4	25.6	51.9	52.0
Belgium	23.8	21.4	23.9	26.4	52.3	52.2
Czech Republic	19.6	19.6	25.2	37.1	55.3	43.4
Denmark	39.4	43.6	5.0	5.0	55.5	51.5
Estonia	10.5	14.0	22.4	22.5	67.1	63.5
Finland	32.7	34.8	7.9	9.2	59.4	56.0
France	11.0	28.7	43.4	21.6	45.7	49.7
Germany	22.9	55.2	45.6	13.3	31.5	31.4
Greece	5.1	3.2	0.3	0.3	94.6	96.5
Hungary	4.9	11.3	8.5	3.3	86.6	85.4
Ireland	16.9	15.1	13.8	15.9	69.3	69.0
Italy	8.2	90.8	3.1	4.2	88.8	5.0
Luxembourg	13.9	14.5	42.0	45.9	44.1	39.5
Netherlands	66.6	64.6	4.9	6.6	28.5	28.8
Poland	22.2	21.3	16.3	24.6	61.5	54.1
Portugal	10.5	10.4	1.3	1.6	88.2	88.0
Slovenia	21.2	26.7	6.8	8.9	72.0	64.4
Slovak Republic	11.2	15.0	3.4	8.8	85.4	76.2
Spain	9.2	13.8	1.3	1.5	89.5	84.7
Sweden	15.6	12.1	17.9	18.8	66.4	69.1
United Kingdom	11.0	10.4	12.2	12.3	76.8	77.2
European Union	*14.0*	*34.5*	*12.2*	*10.4*	*73.8*	*55.0*
Iceland	.	32.4	.	28.2	.	39.8
Norway	9.0	26.7	39.2	14.9	51.8	58.4
Switzerland	.	51.8	.	26.0	.	22.3

Note: EU includes only the EU member countries which are also OECD members.

Source: EUROSTAT (2005, 2007), *Farm Structure Survey*,
http://epp.eurostat.ec.europa.eu/portal/page/portal/agriculture/farm_structure.

StatLink ᵃᵍᵖ http://dx.doi.org/10.1787/888933144959

In the European Union, the majority of farmers have acquired their experience through practical work on an agricultural holding. A big part of agricultural training consists of basic training, as only 10% of farm managers have completed full agricultural training. Greece (97%), Portugal (88%), Hungary (86%), Spain (85%) and Slovakia (76%) have the highest share of farmers without any type of agricultural training. In 2010, only two EU-OECD members (the Czech Republic and Luxembourg) registered the highest shares (of more than 30%) of farm managers who have followed a full cycle of agricultural training.

Concerning the provision of government support to education and training to farmers, on average payments made to agricultural schools have increased at higher rates than total support to the sector in the OECD area (**Figure 5.6**). Nevertheless, such support constitutes a very small percentage of total support to the sector.

Figure 5.6 Evolution of payments on agricultural schools and total support to agriculture, OECD area

1990=100

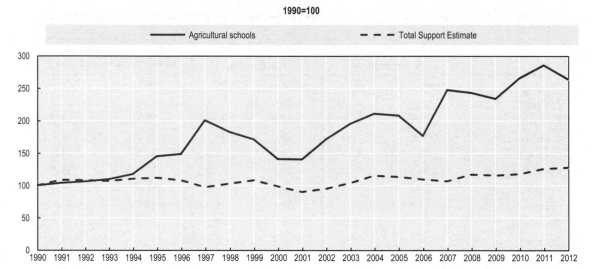

Source: OECD (2013), *"Producer and Consumer Support Estimates"*, *OECD Agriculture Statistics Database*, http://dx.doi.org/10.1787/agr-pcse-data-en.

StatLink http://dx.doi.org/10.1787/888933144803

An important feature of structural change in agriculture in OECD countries is the general ageing of the farming population. This trend is caused by the combined effect of the low exit rate from farming of elderly farmers and the low entrance rate of young farmers.

Across the European Union, for example, the overall number of young farmers has decreased significantly, while the number of older farmers has decreased only marginally, thereby augmenting the share of elderly farmers in the workforce (**Table 5.5**). These figures suggest that elderly farmers are not retiring and passing on their farms to younger generations at a rate that would lower the average age of the agricultural workforce sufficiently to facilitate structural change and improve efficiency and innovation.

Generational renewal in agriculture is a precondition for maintaining viable food production and improving competitiveness. New entrants are needed to take over, to invest and to modernise agricultural holdings. Young farmers are better trained and perform better than older farmers in terms of economic potential, farm size, labour productivity and in adopting more environmentally-friendly farm practices.

Young farmers are also more likely to have received a full agricultural training. In the European Union, while 17% of farmers under the age of 35 have had full agricultural training, more than 80% of farmers between 55 and 64 years acquired their knowledge from practical experience. Attracting new entrants to a sector in a coherent and comprehensive manner is a major policy challenge.

Table 5.5. Share of young and elderly farmers in some EU member states

	1990	2000	2005	2007	2010	1990	2000	2005	2007	2010
Austria		16	12	10	11			10		8
Belgium		11	7	6	5			20		20
Czech Republic			10	10	12			17		13
Denmark	11	10	7	6	5	20		18	20	19
Estonia			7	6	7			28		28
Finland		11	9	9	9			6		10
France	13	10	9	8	9	14		14	13	12
Germany		17	9	8	7			7		5
Greece	9	9	7	7	7	25		36	36	33
Hungary			8	8	7			27		29
Ireland		13	11	7	7			21		25
Italy	5	5	3	3	5	31		41	43	37
Luxembourg	13	11	8	5	7	14		14	14	14
Netherlands	11	7	5	4	4	14		17	18	18
Poland			13	12	15			17		8
Portugal	7	4	2	2	3	28		46	47	46
Slovenia			4	4	4			34		30
Slovak Republic			4	4	7			29		23
Spain	8	9	6	4	5	21		31	31	30
Sweden		7	6	5	5			20		26
United Kingdom		5	4	3	4			27		28
EU-15		8		5	6					

Source: EUROSTAT, *Farm Structure Survey*, 1990, 2007, 2010.
http://epp.eurostat.ec.europa.eu/portal/page/portal/agriculture/farm_structure.

StatLink ᴍᴤ⊓ http://dx.doi.org/10.1787/888933144965

Investing in green innovation

In most countries for which data are available, the public sector plays a major role in agricultural R&D. Expressing agricultural R&D expenditures as a percentage of total research expenditure provides an indication of the relative importance given to research on agriculture within the constraints imposed by overall public spending on research. **Figure 5.7** shows that that there is a wide disparity across countries in the amount of government R&D expenditure devoted to the agricultural sector. These percentages vary from about one-fifth in New Zealand to around 2% in Belgium. The empirical evidence also suggests that the share of the government R&D budget devoted to agriculture has remained relatively stable in the OECD area in the last two decades, at around 3% of the total.

Business expenditures on agricultural R&D also account for a small share of total business R&D in most OECD countries for which data are available, with one exception: New Zealand which has the largest share (7%). The share of most of the remaining countries for which data are available is less than 2% (**Figure 5.8**). However, the share of the agricultural sector in public R&D is larger, and in several cases by a wide margin, than the sector's contribution to total GDP, implying that agricultural R&D expenditures are well maintained.

Figure 5.7. Government budget appropriations or outlays for R&D (GBAORD): Share of agriculture, 2010-12, (%)

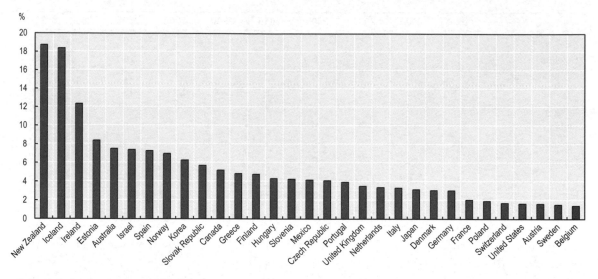

Note: Data for the average 2010-12 refer to the average 2010-11 for Belgium, Estonia, France, Hungary, Israel, Korea, Mexico, Slovenia, Spain, Sweden and the United Kingdom; to the year 2010 for New Zealand and Switzerland. ISCIC REV 4.

Source: OECD (2013), *OECD Research and Development Statistics – GBAORD by Socio-economic Objective (*Science, Technology and Patents Database*).*
http://stats.oecd.org/Index.aspx?DataSetCode=GBAORD_NABS2007.

StatLink ᓕᔑᐧ *http://dx.doi.org/10.1787/888933144817*

Figure 5.8. Business enterprises R&D expenditure: Share of agriculture in total, 2010 or more recent year

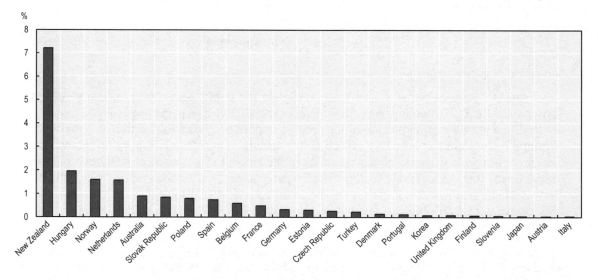

Note: Data for the average 2010-12 refer to the average 2010-11 for Belgium, Estonia, France, Hungary, Israel, Korea, Mexico, Slovenia, Spain, Sweden and the United Kingdom; to the year 2010 for New Zealand and Switzerland. ISCIC REV 4.
Source: OECD (2013), *OECD Research and Development Statistics – GBAORD by Socio-economic Objective (*Science, Technology and Patents Database*).*
http://stats.oecd.org/Index.aspx?DataSetCode=GBAORD_NABS2007.

StatLink ᓕᔑᐧ *http://dx.doi.org/10.1787/888933144820*

Nevertheless, juxtaposing public agricultural R&D expenditures against support to the sector, as measured by the Total Support Estimate, suggests that agricultural R&D expenditures are modest compared to other types of expenditures (**Figure 5.9**). In absolute terms, R&D for the OECD area as a whole has recorded a steady increase, while the TSE has declined or slightly increased over 1990-2012 (**Figure 5.10**).

Figure 5.9. Share of agricultural R&D payments in total support to agriculture, 2010-12

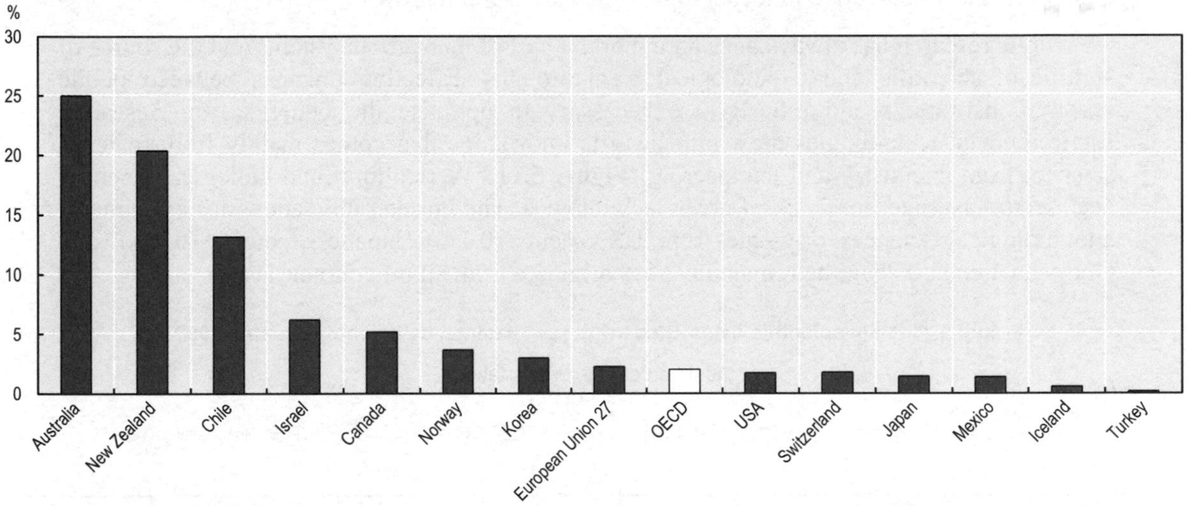

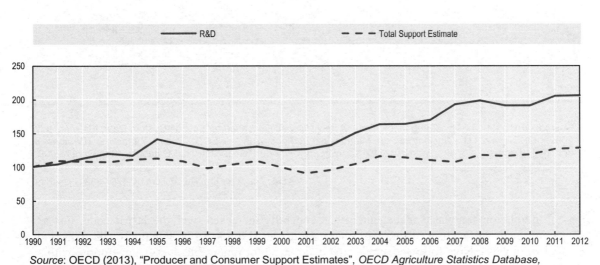

Source: OECD (2013), "Producer and Consumer Support Estimates", *OECD Agriculture Statistics Database*, http://dx.doi.org/10.1787/agr-pcse-data-en.

StatLink ⬛ℿℿ️ http://dx.doi.org/10.1787/888933144831

Figure 5.10. Evolution of agricultural R&D payments and total support to agriculture, OECD area

1990=100

Source: OECD (2013), "Producer and Consumer Support Estimates", *OECD Agriculture Statistics Database*, http://dx.doi.org/10.1787/agr-pcse-data-en.

StatLink ⬛ℿℿ️ http://dx.doi.org/10.1787/888933144840

OECD work on green innovation indicates that green technology development is accelerating in all areas (OECD, 2013b). Since 1990, the share of green patents has been increasing in most regions and countries, reaching 10% of total patents in 2010 (OECD, 2011). This is partly due to increased innovations related to technologies and optimisation processes that support cleaner energy generation and increased efficiency. Moreover, most of the technology development is concentrated in a relatively small number of countries. In general, OECD countries with the highest all-purpose innovation are also among the most innovative in technologies relevant to green growth.

Public research has always been an important part of innovation systems and the source of significant scientific and technological breakthroughs. Effective linkages between public research institutions and industry are necessary to optimise the benefits from research. Environmental technologies draw on scientific knowledge that comes mainly from material science, from chemistry and engineering (**Figure 5.11**). Agricultural and biological sciences account, on average, for 3.7% of green technologies. The link to publications for agricultural and biological sciences originate from US patents (0.7%), Japanese patents (0.3%), and German patents (0.2%); the remaining 2.5% originate from all other countries

Figure 5.11. Main scientific fields cited in "green" patents, by inventor country, 2000-07

As a percentage of all citations

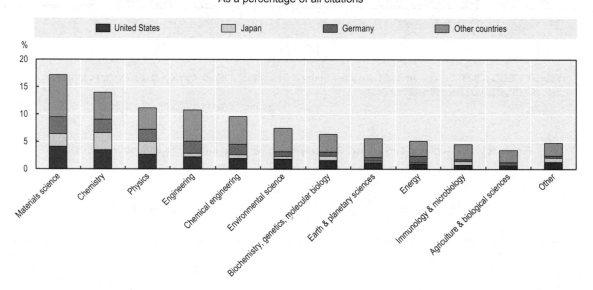

Source: OECD (2010), *Measuring Innovation – A new Perspective*, based on Scopus Custom Data, Elsevier, July 2009; OECD (2011), "Indicators of international co-operation", *OECD Patent Statistics* (Database). doi: 10.1787/data-00507-en, January 2010; and EPO, Worldwide Patent Statistical Database, September 2009, https://data.epo.org/data.html.

StatLink ᵃᵍ⊟ http://dx.doi.org/10.1787/888933144859

Innovation for waste management has generally increased over the last decade, just as patent levels in fertilisers from waste have decreased (**Figure 5.12**). Patents for biofuels and fuel from waste have followed similar trends to those for renewable energy generation, with a steady increase over 1999-2009 and a subsequent decrease in 2010 (by 50%). Evidence at the plant level shows large differences in innovation efforts across countries (**Figure 5.13**).

Figure 5.12. Patents in environment-related technologies in agriculture, OECD area (1999=100)

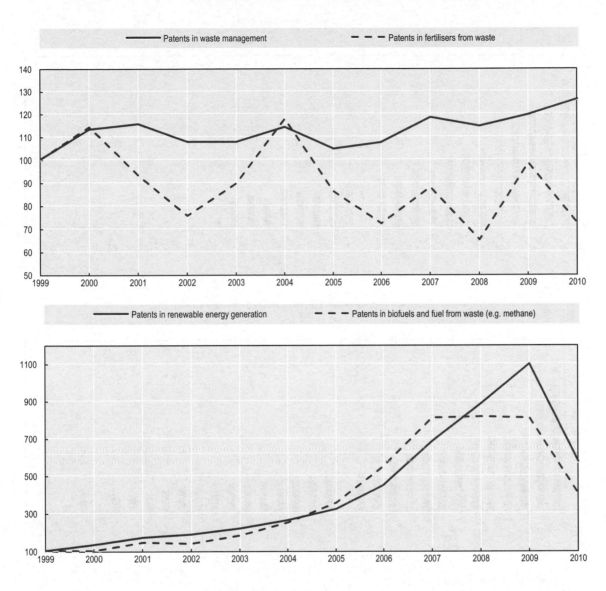

Source: OECD (2011), "Patents by Main Technology and by International Patent Classification (IPC)", OECD *Patent Statistics* (database). http://doi/10.1787/data-00508-en, (accessed on 8 July 2013).

StatLink 🔢 *http://dx.doi.org/10.1787/888933144863*

Figure 5.13. Patents in environmentally-related technologies in agriculture, 2008-10

Share in waste management[1] (%)

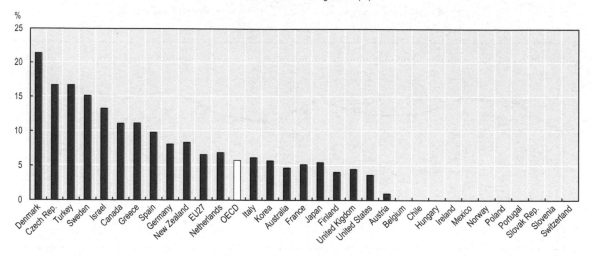

Share in energy generation from renewable and non-fossil sources[2] (%)

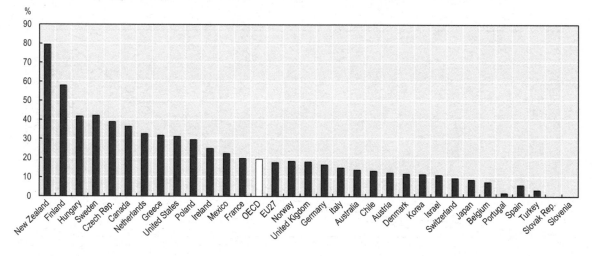

1. Refers to the share of fertilisers from waste.
2. Refers to the share of biofuels and fuel from waste (e.g. methane).

Source: OECD (2011), "Patents by Main Technology and by International Patent Classification (IPC)", OECD *Patent Statistics* (database). http://doi/10.1787/data-00508-en, (accessed 8 July 2013).

StatLink ᴍᴦᴤ http://dx.doi.org/10.1787/888933144870

Concerning trends and patterns of innovation (as measured by patents) in water-related agricultural technologies, such as drip irrigation, drought-resistant crops and controlled watering, these have increased steadily over the last decades (**Figure 5.14**). Drought-resistant crop technologies experienced the highest rate of growth, with very high growth at the end of the 1990s and the beginning of the 2000s, before flattening towards the end of that decade.

Innovation in water-related technologies appears to be concentrated in a handful of countries. World-wide, the United States is by far the front-runner in innovations in agricultural water technologies, while certain countries have achieved strong positions in specific fields (OECD, 2013a).

Figure 5.14. Trends of water-related innovations in agriculture

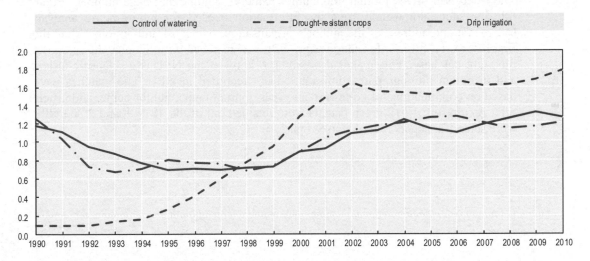

Note: To make the series comparable, they have been normalised by their own average.
Source: Dechezleprêtre, A., I. Haščič and N. Johnstone (2013), "Invention and International Diffusion of Water Conservation and Availability Technologies: Evidence from Patent Data", in OECD (2013), *International Cooperation for Climate Innovation: A problem Shared is a Problem Halved*, OECD report, Paris.

StatLink ⟨≡⊓⟩ http://dx.doi.org/10.1787/888933144889

Notes

1.   Reference levels define the minimum level of environmental quality that farmers are obliged to provide at their own expense and differ from country to country depending on property rights and legal systems (OECD 2010).

2.   This aspect of indicators will benefit from the on-going work to refine the OECD Green Growth indicators.

3.   The approach taken to defining environmental taxes in the SEEA differs from the approach commonly found in the economics literature where environmental taxes are defined with reference to taxing negative externalities (i.e. Pigouvian taxes). These types of taxes are based on an assessment of the motive for setting rates of tax (i.e. the extent to which a particular tax rate will reduce the negative externality). Pigouvian taxes do not include taxes collected for fiscally motivated reasons. Since determining the precise motivation for taxation presents a difficult measurement issue, the focus in the SEEA is to consider the underlying tax base.

4.   Most domestic prices in New Zealand are aligned with world prices and payments are only provided for animal disease control and relief in the event of large scale natural disasters.

5.   For a detailed definition of the potentially most environmentally beneficial support, see Table 3.1 in OECD (2013a).

6.   R&D expenditure can also be expressed as a percentage of agricultural GDP (research intensity ratios) to capture agricultural research efforts (see OECD, 1995).

7.   These data are included in the payments in the Producer Support Estimate (PSE).

8. The listed NPL gives journal title, author name(s), volume and page number, article title, but does not usually give the information needed for biblio-metric analysis (e.g. name and address of the author's organisation, names of authors other than the first listed). To fill in information gaps, NPL was matched with Scopus, the scientific literature database. This makes it possible to know if the NPL is a scientific article and to obtain bibliographical information not recorded in NPL. The matches were based on combinations of volume, page, year, journal name, author name, and article title. As a result, 1 612 green patents were retained out of the 48 249, and 2 803 NPL were scientific papers recorded in Scopus.

Bibliography

Australian Bureau of Statistics (ABS) (2013), *Towards the Australian Environmental-Economic Accounts*, Information Paper, Canberra.

Dechezleprêtre, A., I. Haščič and N. Johnstone (2013), "Invention and International Diffusion of Water Conservation and Availability Technologies: Evidence from Patent Data", in OECD (2013), *International Co-operation for Climate Innovation: A problem Shared is a Problem Halved*, OECD report, Paris.

EUROSTAT, *Farm Structure Survey*, 1990, 2007, 2010, http://epp.eurostat.ec.europa.eu/portal/page/portal/agriculture/farm_structure.

Labarthe, P. and C. Laurent (2009), *Transformations of agricultural extension services in the EU: towards a lack of adequate knowledge for small-scale farms.* Paper presented at the 111 EAAE-IAAE seminar "Small farms: decline or persistence", University of Kent 26-27 June, http://ageconsearch.umn.edu/bitstream/52859/2/103.pdf.

OECD (2014), *Green Growth Indicators 2014*, OECD Green Growth Studies, OECD Publishing, Paris, doi: http://dx.doi.org/10.1787/9789264202030-en.

OECD (2013a), *Policy Instruments to Support Green Growth in Agriculture; A Synthesis of Country Experiences,* OECD Publishing, Paris, http://dx.doi.org/10.1787/9789264203525-en.

OECD (2013b), *Agricultural Innovation Systems: A Framework for Analysing the Role of the Government*, OECD Publishing, Paris, DOI: http://dx.doi.org/10.1787/9789264200593-en.

OECD (2013c), *Taxing Energy Use: A Graphical Analysis*, OECD Publishing, Paris, doi: http://dx.doi.org/10.1787/9789264183933-en.

OECD (2012a), *Agricultural Policy Monitoring and Evaluation 2012: OECD Countries*, OECD Publishing, Paris, doi: http://dx.doi.org/10.1787/agr_pol-2012-en

OECD (2012b), *New Sources of Growth - Knowledge-Based Capital Driving Investment and Productivity in the 21st Century. Interim Project Findings*, OECD report, Paris. http://www.oecd.org/sti/50498841.pdf

OECD (2011), *Towards Green Growth: Monitoring Progress: OECD Indicators*, OECD Green Growth Studies, OECD Publishing. Paris, doi: http://dx.doi.org/10.1787/9789264111356-en.

OECD (2010), *Sustainable Management of Water Resources in Agriculture*, OECD report, Paris, www.oecd.org/tad/sustainable-agriculture/sustainablemanagementofwaterresourcesinagriculture.htm.

OECD (2009), *Patent Statistics Manual*, OECD report, Paris, www.oecd.org/science/inno/oecdpatentstatisticsmanual.htm.

OECD (1995), *Technological Change and Structural Adjustment in OECD Agriculture*, OECD report, Paris.

United Nations (UN) (2014), *System of Environmental Economic Accounting – Central Framework*, European Commission, FAO, IMF, OECD, UN, the World Bank, United Nations, New York, http://unstats.un.org/unsd/envaccounting/seeaRev/SEEA_CF_Final_en.pdf.

ORGANISATION FOR ECONOMIC CO-OPERATION AND DEVELOPMENT

The OECD is a unique forum where governments work together to address the economic, social and environmental challenges of globalisation. The OECD is also at the forefront of efforts to understand and to help governments respond to new developments and concerns, such as corporate governance, the information economy and the challenges of an ageing population. The Organisation provides a setting where governments can compare policy experiences, seek answers to common problems, identify good practice and work to co-ordinate domestic and international policies.

The OECD member countries are: Australia, Austria, Belgium, Canada, Chile, the Czech Republic, Denmark, Estonia, Finland, France, Germany, Greece, Hungary, Iceland, Ireland, Israel, Italy, Japan, Korea, Luxembourg, Mexico, the Netherlands, New Zealand, Norway, Poland, Portugal, the Slovak Republic, Slovenia, Spain, Sweden, Switzerland, Turkey, the United Kingdom and the United States. The European Union takes part in the work of the OECD.

OECD Publishing disseminates widely the results of the Organisation's statistics gathering and research on economic, social and environmental issues, as well as the conventions, guidelines and standards agreed by its members.

OECD PUBLISHING, 2, rue André-Pascal, 75775 PARIS CEDEX 16
(51 2014 08 1 P) ISBN 978-92-64-22317-2 – 2014-02